© 2025 Centurion Publishing Group

TABLE OF CONTENTS

INTRODUCTION — 1

IT WASN'T MUCH, BUT IT MATTERED. — 4

THE CURRENCY OF STRUGGLE — 8

PERSISTANCE — 12

IT'S YOUR FAULT. — 18

THE STILLNESS WE NEED — 21

ANXIETY — 26

PROCRASTINATION — 31

WHEN IT COUNTS, SKILLS MATTER — 35

MAKE CAPABLE COOL AGAIN — 44

YOU ARE THE APEX — 48

THE CRUCIBLE OF FAILURE — 53

THE RAZOR'S EDGE OF SIMPLICITY — 59

WHAT YOU PROTECT, REVEALS — 64
WHO YOU ARE.

NOTES ON LEADERSHIP — 72

THE PARADOX OF COMMUNICATION — 79

THE PITFALL TEST — 83

FAMILY BY CHOICE — 89

KNOW YOURSELF FIRST	97
EARN YOUR GOOSEBUMPS	104
ON HAPPINESS	109
BEAUTY IN THE BROKEN PLACES	114
THE EDGE REMAINS	123
ACKNOWLEDGMENTS	128

INTRODUCTION

When you hold an arrowhead in your hand, you're holding a story. Not just a piece of stone, but the record of every strike that gave it shape. At first glance it looks ordinary, a shard of flint or obsidian that could be mistaken for debris. But if you look closer, the story reveals itself. The fractures. The ridges. The edges that catch the light. None of it is accidental. Each mark is the memory of pressure applied in the right place, at the right angle, repeated until the stone gave in to purpose.

No two arrowheads are the same. Each one carries a different pattern of scars, a different history of strikes, a different edge. Their value isn't in looking perfect, it's in being sharp, ready, and proven by the marks they carry. A crisp dollar bill may look clean, but it's still worth less than a torn and stained hundred. What matters is not condition, but what can be carried into use.

The arrowhead didn't begin sharp. It wasn't useful at first. It became that way through failure, patience, and persistence. Its scars are what define it. Every scar is a receipt: proof that the world demanded something from you, and you paid in full.

That image has stayed with me because it isn't just about stone. It's about people.

I know because I've carried my own fractures. Some came from mistakes I couldn't take back. Some from losses I couldn't prevent. Some from responsibilities I wasn't ready for but had to shoulder anyway. Those moments left marks, and for a long time I thought they were proof of weakness. They weren't. They were the strikes that gave me shape. Every one of us is being shaped by something. We all begin rough, unformed, and ordinary. What defines us is the pressure we face, the fractures we endure, and what we allow them to make of us. Some grow sharp, capable, and defined by their scars. Others are dulled, worn smooth by comfort and neglect. Life will leave its mark either way. The only question is whether those marks leave you sharp enough to endure what comes.

This book is built on that idea. It isn't a manual or a blueprint. It's closer to a quiver — a set of reflections and lessons you can draw from one at a time, in no particular order, whenever you need them. Some are personal. Others are observations about the world. All circle the same truth: our edges are earned, not given.

We live in a time when nearly every form of discomfort can be avoided. Food arrives instantly. Entertainment is always within reach. Comfort is sold as the highest form of living. But ease has consequences. It erodes character. It makes people fragile. Comfort is counterfeit strength. It feels solid until the first strike shatters it. And fragility is not harmless. It leaves us dependent, vulnerable, and incapable of standing when we are needed most.

History didn't prepare us for this. For most of human existence, struggle wasn't optional. It was daily reality. People hunted, built, endured weather, and buried loved ones too soon. The world sharpened them whether they wanted it to or not. Today, for the first time, it's possible to drift through life without ever being tested. And yet the tests still come. Storms don't wait for us to prepare. They break against us all the same.

If you've already been shaped by hardship, you know the weight it leaves behind. Maybe you've carried failure. Maybe you've endured loss. Maybe you've shouldered responsibility for someone else's safety, or had to answer for mistakes when there was nowhere to hide. Those moments leave marks.

Or maybe you feel the opposite — that somewhere along the way, comfort dulled you, and you're left with the suspicion that you wouldn't stand as firm as you'd like when tested. That isn't weakness. It's awareness. And awareness is the first strike that begins to shape you.

The pages ahead are written for both kinds of people: those who already know the weight of scars, and those who sense they need to sharpen themselves before the test comes. These reflections won't give you shortcuts. They won't hand you perfection. What they will give you are edges — fragments of truth to carry into the fight, reminders forged from struggle, persistence, responsibility, and endurance.

And that is the point: the edge is everything. When the storm comes, no one will ask what you meant to be. They'll see only whether you are sharp enough to stand. That sharpness cannot be borrowed. It cannot be faked. It must be earned. These are your earned edges.

IT WASN'T MUCH, BUT IT MATTERED.

Most people expect the moments that change their life to be loud.

They think there's going to be a dramatic turning point. Something cinematic. A fight that ends everything, a breakthrough conversation that heals it, a heroic decision that alters the course of a mission, or a handshake across a polished conference table that signals success. We've been trained to look for big moments. Trained to believe that clarity and transformation show up with background music, perfect lighting, and instant resolution.

You see it everywhere. In movies, in books, in the way people tell their own stories. The narrative is always clean. Cause, effect, revelation. You're supposed to know when everything changes. You're supposed to feel it deep in your chest and walk away somehow different. People spend years chasing that version of life. They wait for it. They expect it. And they feel lost or disappointed when it never shows up.

But that version of reality is a lie.

In the real world, the things that shape you don't usually feel important while they're happening. They're quiet. Unremarkable. You only notice them when you look back, and by then, the moment's gone. You realize the argument didn't end the relationship. It was already eroding because of the things you both stopped doing long before that. You realize the operation didn't succeed because of some last-minute brilliance. It went well because everything was checked, cleaned, confirmed, and handled without hesitation. You realize the deal didn't close because of your pitch. It closed because the other person never had to second-guess your follow-through.

Whether we're talking about personal relationships, tactical operations, or business deals, the truth is the same. Success and failure are never about one big decision. They're about a hundred small ones. The ones that don't feel like they matter. The ones you think you can skip. The ones no one will notice until they're not done right.

The little things aren't little. They just feel that way at the time. But if you stack enough of them, they become the whole story.

You see it in relationships first. Not the Instagram version, not the once-a-year vacation or the grand romantic gesture. Real, day-to-day relationships. The ones that last. They're not built on big moments. They're built on tone, on timing, on whether or not you're still paying attention. Most people don't fall apart because of some explosive event. They drift. They stop listening. They stop softening their voice when they're stressed. They stop noticing what used to be obvious. And all of those little shifts, ignored or brushed off, start to erode the ground underneath. It happens slowly, but it's real. And once it takes hold, it's hard to reverse.

The same thing applies when the stakes are higher. In the tactical world, failure rarely shows up as a single disaster. When something goes wrong, it usually started hours or days before, back when something routine got skipped. Gear didn't get checked. A comms test was missed. A team member wasn't fully dialed in and no one said anything. You don't lose control all at once. You bleed it out, step by step, by treating familiar processes like they don't matter. And when it finally shows up, it's too late to fix. You're not preventing anymore. You're managing fallout.

On the other side, when things go smooth, it's rarely dramatic. It's quiet. Efficient. Everything's been handled. No chaos, no surprises. That kind of outcome isn't luck. It's the result of a mindset that takes the smallest details seriously, not because someone's watching, but because that's the standard. You don't get to cut corners in this world. The cost of failure is too high.

And then there's business, which looks different but operates the same way underneath. Deals don't fall apart because of one misstep. They unravel quietly. A delayed reply. A promise that doesn't get followed up on. A pattern of being just a little too loose with the details. That kind of thing builds just like anything else. The person on the other end starts to feel it. Starts to lose confidence. Starts to look elsewhere. And by the time you realize what's happening, the opportunity is already gone.

But it works the other way too. The people who keep showing up, keep doing what they say, keep catching the things no one else catches, they stand out. Not with flash. With consistency. And that's what builds reputation. Not charisma. Not performance. Just care, over and over again, until it's clear this is who you are, not just how you act when it's convenient.

No matter the arena, it's never about a single event. It's the pattern. It's how seriously you take the small things, and whether you let them slip once you think you've arrived. The little things don't feel like much while they're happening. But they're the difference between stable ground and a slow collapse.

You don't get to know which moment is going to matter most. That's the part no one tells you. It won't come with a warning. It won't feel significant while it's happening. It might even feel forgettable. Until one day, you realize that was the moment everything held together, or the moment it quietly started to fall apart.

And by then, it's already part of your story.

So be the person who takes the small things seriously. Not because someone's watching. Not because it's impressive.

But because it's the only way to live a life that holds up under pressure.

Most people don't fall into one big collapse. They leak. Quietly. Slowly. One overlooked detail at a time.

Don't be one of them.

THE CURRENCY OF STRUGGLE

I've been wrestling with something lately. A quiet frustration that stuck around long enough to deserve a closer look.

It shows up when someone close to me says they're overwhelmed. Burnt out. Maxed out. And I know they mean it, but part of me instinctively compares it to what I've been carrying. That's where the resentment starts.

Most days, I'm balancing multiple businesses, complex problems, and constant decision-making. Not because I'm chasing prestige, but because it's the only structure that works for me. I've spent years moving from one demanding project to another, and I function best when I'm under load. If I slow down, I drift. My brain doesn't do "idle".

So I built a life around momentum. It works, but it also makes it hard to relate. When someone talks about how exhausted they are from a relatively light schedule, I catch myself pulling away. Not because I don't care, but because the mismatch between our definitions of effort becomes hard to ignore.

Letting that frustration build turns connection into calculation. It makes the people around you feel smaller than they are, and your own work feels bitter instead of meaningful. I've felt that shift, and I don't want to live there.

This isn't just a personal issue. It happens everywhere. Relationships. Teams. Even tight-knit units where trust is everything. It creeps in when people start treating stress like a badge of honor, exaggerating effort for sympathy or status. If it goes unchecked, it fractures everything.

Somewhere along the way, exhaustion became a kind of

social currency. You're not just valuable for what you do, but for how loudly you suffer through it. If you're someone who works in silence, you notice that. You notice who needs their grind to be recognized, who needs the struggle seen more than the results.

It's not always intentional. Most people aren't gaming the system. But when you carry more than you speak on, and someone else broadcasts every burden, it wears on you. It starts to feel like you live in a different world.

Research backs this up. A study in the Journal of Applied Psychology showed that people tend to overestimate their own workload compared to others, especially in team settings. That bias makes everyone feel like they're doing the most, even when they're not. So while some are venting out loud, others are internalizing that imbalance quietly.

That's when you start keeping score.

And that's when it gets dangerous.

Resentment rarely announces itself. It shows up as distance. You stop offering ideas. You stop initiating. You stop trusting that the other person really knows what pressure feels like. By the time you notice, the connection already feels compromised.

I've felt that. I've heard someone complain about being slammed and nodded, all while thinking about the twenty things I handled before lunch. I didn't say anything, but I started seeing them differently. Not as a teammate, but as someone I couldn't count on. That's the fracture point, when empathy gets replaced by judgment.

And once it sets in, even small interactions feel charged. Every complaint sounds like a dig. Every moment of venting sounds like theater. The issue stops being about work. It becomes a question of trust.

The hard truth is that waiting for resentment to speak for you never works. It doesn't fix the dynamic. It just poisons it. If you want to prevent that drift, you have to stay ahead of it.

That means owning your limits. If you naturally take on more, that's fine, but don't use that as an excuse to stay silent and build resentment. Say when things aren't sustainable. You don't need permission to protect your bandwidth.

It also means watching for patterns. If someone always positions themselves as the most overwhelmed, pay attention. Not to judge, but to decide how close you want to stand when their narrative starts shaping reality.

And if you're the quiet one, stop wearing that silence like a badge. I used to think not saying anything made me strong. All it really did was make me feel alone. People can't respect what they can't see. If you're at capacity, say it. That's not weakness. That's honesty.

Maybe the biggest shift is redefining what hard work looks like. Just because someone talks about their stress more doesn't mean they're doing more. And just because you don't say anything doesn't mean you're fine. Know the difference between humility and invisibility. One earns respect. The other eats away at it.

This isn't about being tougher. It's about protecting what matters before resentment ruins it.

I don't expect everyone to move at my pace. That's not realistic. But I do expect honesty. I expect people to live in reality, not in a burnout theater. And I need to hold myself to that same standard.

Because when struggle becomes currency, the whole system breaks. People inflate their pain, downplay others' effort, and let resentment take the place of trust. That's not something I want to be part of.

So now, I stay sharp on both sides. I check my story before I question someone else's. I speak up before frustration sets in. And I remind myself that real connection isn't about who works the hardest. It's about being honest about what we carry.

PERSISTANCE

If there's one principle that's shaped my life more than any other, it's persistence.

Not talent. Not intelligence. Not luck, charm, or timing. Just the simple decision to keep going when everything in you wants to stop. The ability to show up, again and again, whether it's noticed or not. The quiet force that keeps you moving forward through failure, fatigue, and frustration.

There's a quote I've kept close for years. People often credit it to Calvin Coolidge. Whether or not he wrote it is something we'll explore, but the authorship has never mattered to me. What matters is how true it is, and how much it explains.

> **Nothing in this world can take the place of persistence.**
>
> **Talent will not; nothing is more common than unsuccessful men with talent.**
>
> **Genius will not; unrewarded genius is almost a proverb.**
>
> **Education will not; the world is full of educated derelicts.**
>
> **Persistence and determination alone are omnipotent.**
>
> **The slogan 'Press On!' has solved and always will solve the problems of the human race.**

I've watched talented people walk away. I've seen brilliant thinkers stall out and go quiet. I've known highly educated people who never applied what they knew because they were too afraid to risk failure. The people who endure, the ones who build something meaningful, are rarely the most gifted. They're the ones who don't stop.

This isn't about forced optimism. It's not about pretending hardship doesn't sting. It's about what it really means to push forward when nothing feels certain. It's about the kind of persistence that doesn't shout or perform, but outlasts. The kind that doesn't rely on being motivated. The kind that just works.

This write up is the foundation. It's the place I'll point to whenever someone asks how to keep going. It's the heart of how I operate, how I lead, and how I repair the pieces when everything falls apart.

If you take only one thing from this book, let it be this. Press on.

Most people think the quote comes from Calvin Coolidge, and on the surface, that makes sense. He was quiet, disciplined, and believed in staying out of the spotlight. The quote reflects that kind of thinking. But he didn't write it.

The earliest version of the message came from a minister named Theodore T. Munger in 1881. His writing focused more on the power of purpose than persistence, but the tone and message were familiar. Later, in the early 1900s, a man named Edward Hart, speaking at a life insurance convention, shaped the quote into something closer to what we know today. He sharpened the language, added the contrast with talent and education, and introduced the phrase "Press On."

By the late 1920s, newspapers had started printing versions of the quote and attributing them to Coolidge. He didn't argue. In fact, after his presidency, he included the quote in materials for New York Life, which helped solidify the connection.

He didn't come up with it. But he embraced it. And while his presidency may not have left a powerful mark, the quote has. It outlasted him, just like the message promises.

That's what matters.

The reason this quote sticks is because it strips away all the excuses. It doesn't care where you went to school, how smart you are, or how much potential you had. It only cares whether or not you kept going.

Talent is common. So is wasted talent. Intelligence without action doesn't build anything. And education, no matter how expensive or impressive, is useless without follow-through. The world is full of people who could have done something if they had just stuck with it.

Persistence is rare. That's why it's powerful. And it's rare because it's hard.

Continuing when you're tired, discouraged, or humiliated is one of the hardest things a person can do. It means showing up when no one's watching, when the outcome is uncertain, and when failure feels personal. Most people can't do that consistently. They start strong, get excited, and fall off the minute it gets boring or painful. That's the pattern.

If you can break that pattern, even a little, you already have an edge; Not because you're better, not because you know more, just because you're still in the fight when most people have already walked away.

Persistence is not glamorous, but it is the deciding factor more often than anything else. The longer you can hold the line, the more the odds tilt in your favor. That's the truth no one wants to hear, because it means the path forward is hard and slow.

But it also means the path is wide open. Most people won't take it. That's your advantage.

Persistence is the great equalizer.

You can't choose where you're born, who raises you, or what kind of start you get. Life hands people wildly different circumstances, and pretending otherwise is dishonest. Some people are born with advantages — some aren't. But persistence is the one variable anyone can control.

It doesn't matter if you're broke, behind, or starting from scratch. The one thing you can always do is refuse to quit. You can decide that no matter how many times you get knocked down, you'll get back up. That choice is available to everyone; And because so few people make it, it becomes a weapon.

You don't have to be the smartest. You don't have to be the fastest. You don't even have to be the most skilled. If you outlast the others, if you keep showing up after they've stopped, you change the outcome. That's how people with no background, no support, and no obvious advantage still win.

The world can stack the odds against you, but if you never stop pushing, it has to give ground. Eventually, something breaks. Eventually, the pressure you apply creates movement. That's what persistence does. It doesn't ask for permission, it just keeps going until there's no choice but progress.

That's what makes it powerful. That's what makes it fair.

I didn't come into the defense industry the way most people did.

Most had a traditional path. They came from the right background, had the right experience, or followed a standard track that opened doors for them. I didn't have that. I started young, without the pedigree, and without the resume that would make people say yes on paper.

What I had was persistence.

Since I couldn't walk through the front door, I had to build my own way in. That meant grinding, learning, acquiring a clearance, and stacking qualifications. Not for attention or approval, but because I knew it was the only way. I had to outwork the process. I had to make it undeniable.

Eventually, someone saw that effort. A friend who understood what I was trying to do. His name was Curtis. He saw how long I had been clawing my way forward and gave me a shot; Not a handout, not a shortcut, just an opportunity to prove I had earned a place.

That chance changed everything. It was the beginning of a career built entirely on staying in the fight. And I will never be able to thank him enough for it; not just for the opportunity, but for the example. He let me prove that I could do it the hard way. And he did it too, every single day.

I will spend the rest of my life trying to live up to that example.

Everyone wants a shortcut. They want a secret, a hack, or a system. They want to believe there is something out there that explains why others succeed while they are still stuck. But most of the time, it is none of those things. It is not brilliance, it is not luck, it is not perfect timing —It is persistence.

Persistence is not loud, it is not exciting, it is not even inspiring most of the time. It is quiet and unglamorous. It looks like doing the work when no one cares. It feels like moving forward when nothing is working. It means getting back up when you are exhausted, unsure, or alone. That is the truth most people do not want to hear.

But it is the truth that actually matters.

If you are willing to stay in the fight, when others give up, the gap starts to form. You do not have to be the most gifted, you do not have to be the best, you just have to be there when everyone else has stopped. That is what changes everything.

This is not theory, it is not motivation. It is the core of what separates people who endure from people who fade out. It is the reason someone with no connections, no formal background, and nothing handed to them can still build something great. And it is available to anyone.

If there is one thing I want to be remembered for, it is not being talented, it is not being impressive, it is this. I did not quit. I kept showing up, I pressed on.

And if you do the same, nothing can stop you.

Press on.

This chapter is dedicated to my friend Curtis who gave me a chance when no one else would. He saw the work, the effort, and the intent, and he opened the door. He didn't have to, but he did.

He was killed in the line of duty in 2017. I will never stop striving to be the kind of man he was. Loyal, quietly strong and relentless. A true warrior in every sense.

I owe him more than I can say.

IT'S YOUR FAULT.

Not because a Navy SEAL said so on a podcast. Not because you're supposed to wake up at four in the morning and punish yourself into greatness. Not because you need to drag around other people's mistakes like penance.

This isn't martyrdom. It isn't guilt. Accountability is about clarity.

A friend of mine, Carlos, once told me a story from his trip to Italy. He was standing in line with a guy who wouldn't stop complaining about his flight. Long lines. Bad service. No room in the seats. Carlos let him finish, then said, "It's your fault. You didn't make enough money to fly private." The guy laughed, but it landed. The complaints vanished, because the frame had shifted. Instead of being a victim of the airline, the man was reminded of the one thing that mattered: his own choices, his own power. He could keep complaining, or he could take ownership and change something.

That's the point. Accountability isn't about guilt. It's about power.

Blame feels natural. We're trained for it. Your boss. The system. Your ex. Your parents. The weather. The algorithm. The list is endless. Point outward, shift the weight, and someone will nod along. People will even praise you for it. They'll tell you you're right, you were mistreated, you deserve better. Sympathy is cheap. Accountability is expensive.

The problem is, blame freezes you in place. It might feel good in the moment, but it doesn't move you forward. Because when you hand away blame, you also hand away power. You give someone else the wheel and then get angry about where the car ends up.

I've done it myself. I've walked away from failed conversations convinced it was all the other person's fault. I've told myself a deal fell through because the other side wasn't serious. Those excuses felt good at the time, but they didn't sharpen me. They didn't change anything. The patterns repeated, because I'd protected my ego instead of facing the truth.

That's what blame is: image management. It makes you feel right without ever making you better.

The loop is easy to spot. Avoid the sting. Rationalize the outcome. Repeat the behavior. Stay stuck.

The only way out is to say, "It's my fault," and mean it. Not as punishment, but as precision. You strip away everything outside your control and look straight at what you could have done differently. Sometimes it's one small thing. Sometimes it's several. But it's yours. And once you see it, the illusion of helplessness disappears. You're not powerless. You're not waiting on someone else. You're holding the lever.

That lever isn't heavy. It just feels sharp because it cuts through excuses. Maybe you stayed too long somewhere you shouldn't have. Maybe you avoided a hard conversation. Maybe you let a standard slide when no one was watching. None of that feels good to admit. But until you do, you'll keep dragging the same problems into the future.

The truth is, most people never get here. They'd rather protect the story than face the sting. They'll say it wasn't fair, or it was someone else's fault, or it couldn't have been avoided. They'll get sympathy, and they'll stay average. Because sympathy doesn't sharpen you. Precision does.

Accountability isn't glamorous. It's quiet. It happens when you sit with yourself and admit the part that was yours. It happens when you choose precision over vagueness. You stop saying, "Everything went wrong," and start saying, "I missed the detail." You stop saying, "They don't get it," and start saying, "I didn't make it clear." Those small shifts are what create different outcomes.

And it's not a one-time choice. It's a posture. Whenever something goes wrong and you're in the room, you own your part. Not more, not less. Just yours. That's enough. And it changes everything, because most people will never do it. They'll keep pointing outward. You'll keep adjusting, refining, moving forward.

You don't need a dramatic ritual. One page is enough. Write down what was in your control. Nothing else. No excuses, no story. Then ask yourself, what lever can I pull so this doesn't happen again? Sometimes it's obvious. Sometimes it's uncomfortable. But it's always there, if you're willing to see it.

That's the secret no one tells you: ownership doesn't weigh you down. It frees you. Because once you stop waiting for others to fix things, you move. You stop drifting. You stop wasting time on fairness and start focusing on what's next. You'll still fail. You'll still make bad calls. You'll still say things you regret. But that doesn't have to be the end of the story. The story is whether you keep reaching for reasons or whether you start reaching for levers.

Blame protects your image. Ownership protects your future.

It's your fault. And that's the best news you'll ever get. Because if it's your fault, it's also your move.

THE STILLNESS WE NEED

We've created a culture where boredom has all but disappeared. Every pause in the day, whether waiting in line, sitting at a red light, or standing in an elevator, is instantly filled by the glow of a screen. The phone comes out of the pocket before the moment can settle, as if silence itself has become unbearable. We tell ourselves this is progress, that we're staying connected, efficient, or entertained. The truth is that by eliminating boredom, we've eliminated one of the most important functions of the human mind.

When the brain is unoccupied, it shifts into what neuroscientists call the default mode network, a system that switches on when we are not focused on a task. It is here that we wander into questions of meaning, wrestle with discomfort, and stumble into our most creative ideas. Yet most of us avoid that space. In one Harvard study, participants were placed alone in a room with nothing to do for fifteen minutes. The only option available was to press a button that delivered a painful electric shock. The majority of people chose the shock over simply sitting with their own thoughts. That is how deeply we fear boredom.

Throughout history, boredom was unavoidable. Farmers worked the same fields year after year, with long hours of repetition broken only by seasons. Sailors spent months at sea with nothing but the horizon and the rhythm of the waves. Soldiers in camp knew that war was not endless action but endless waiting, punctuated by moments of chaos. These stretches of monotony were not wasted; they built resilience, reflection, and patience. Life demanded an ability to sit with stillness.

Writers, thinkers, and artists often leaned into boredom rather than running from it. Blaise Pascal, the French philosopher, famously wrote that "all of humanity's problems stem from man's inability to sit quietly in a room alone." Marcus Aurelius journaled in silence during his campaigns, turning long periods of inactivity into fuel for the philosophy we now call Meditations. Even in religious traditions, silence and stillness have always been disciplines, not punishments — monks sought it, prophets walked into deserts to find it, warriors prepared for battle in meditation before action.

Contrast that with today. We have eliminated the long, empty stretches that shaped human perspective for thousands of years. Where boredom once forged endurance and meaning, we now scramble to erase it with a screen tap. The boredom that was once a teacher has been recast as an enemy.

This resistance comes at a cost. By filling every gap with a screen, we cut ourselves off from the process that forces us to confront the bigger questions, the ones that give life coherence and direction. Those moments of stillness were never meant to be wasted. They were meant to be used.

Boredom hurts. Not in the way of physical pain, but in the way of silence that refuses to be ignored. When the default mode network switches on, the mind drifts toward questions we would rather avoid. What does my life mean? Am I where I thought I would be? Is this all there is? These are not easy thoughts to sit with, and most people spend their lives running from them.

The Harvard study of people shocking themselves rather than sit alone with nothing to do is a perfect mirror of our culture. Given the choice between discomfort and distraction, most will choose distraction every time. The problem is that the cost of avoiding boredom is much greater than the cost of experiencing it. Each time we reach for a screen to drown out stillness, we train ourselves to lose tolerance for reflection. We avoid the very space where growth, clarity, and creativity begin.

The avoidance builds into something larger. When boredom is eliminated, so is the natural mechanism that forces us to wrestle with meaning. Without those moments of silence, the big questions never surface. Over time, that vacuum feeds anxiety, depression, and a sense of hollowness. This isn't abstract—it shows up in the data. Rates of depression and anxiety have soared in step with the rise of constant stimulation. We are overstimulated yet undernourished, bombarded with noise but starved of meaning.

That discomfort you feel in stillness is not a sign that something is wrong. It is a signal that something important is waiting. Boredom is the doorway to meaning, but the doorway is narrow, and it demands that you walk through it rather than look away.

If boredom is painful when we first encounter it, it is also the medicine our minds need. The default mode network, the same system that makes us uncomfortable in silence, is also the one that unlocks perspective and creativity. Give it room to work and it will pull scattered thoughts together, connect ideas that seemed unrelated, and surface answers to questions that usually hide under constant stimulation.

Think about where your best ideas appear. It is rarely in front of a screen. They arrive in the shower, on a run, in the car with no music playing. They show up in the moments when the mind is free to wander. That is not coincidence. It is your brain finally doing the work that constant distraction has been holding back.

The more we allow ourselves to experience boredom, the less threatening it becomes. Ordinary life feels richer when it no longer demands constant entertainment. Work becomes easier to focus on. Relationships feel less strained. Even small routines gain depth because the brain has been retrained to sit with them instead of fleeing from them.

What begins as discomfort turns into clarity, and clarity into meaning.

Boredom will never be glamorous. It is not meant to be. But it is one of the simplest and most reliable ways to reconnect with yourself, and the longer you practice it, the more obvious its value becomes.

The cure only works if it is practiced. Boredom is not something you stumble into anymore. It has to be chosen. That means building deliberate spaces where stillness can exist without being crowded out by a device.

Start simple. Leave your phone at home for a workout. Do not bring a podcast or a playlist. Lift, run, or move in silence and see what surfaces in your head when there is nothing left to distract you. Commute without music or news. Let the drive unfold in quiet and pay attention to the thoughts that arrive. These moments are small, but they retrain the brain to accept stillness instead of fleeing from it.

There are also rules worth setting. Do not sleep with your phone. Do not allow screens at the table when you eat with family or friends. Create boundaries in the evening where the device is set aside and conversation or reflection fills the gap. Take short social media fasts, a day or even a weekend at a time, and notice the withdrawal give way to calm. Each step is a reminder that you are not tethered to the endless scroll, and that life does not collapse when you disconnect.

These are not punishments. They are disciplines. Each one reopens the space we were designed to have. Each one gives the mind back its ability to wander, to create, and to wrestle with meaning.

We live in a time when silence feels foreign and boredom feels like failure. Yet the very moments we rush to avoid are the ones most capable of changing us. Stillness will never compete with the instant gratification of a glowing screen, but it was never meant to. Its purpose is deeper. It draws us back to the questions that matter, the questions that make a life coherent rather than scattered.

You will not find meaning by filling every pause. You will not grow by shocking yourself out of silence. Meaning comes in the quiet, in the places where your thoughts are forced to stretch and your mind is free to wander. The stillness you resist is the stillness you need.

ANXIETY

Anxiety is hard to talk about because most people either overcomplicate it or oversimplify it. They turn it into something mystical, a fog no one can control, or they reduce it to a mechanical problem that a checklist should fix. In my experience it is neither. Anxiety is not random, and it is not solved by slogans. It is quieter, more persistent, and harder to pin down.

Most people assume anxiety shows up during chaos. During the argument. During the fight. During the emergency. That has never been true for me. When things are loud, I usually feel clear. The first time I was shot at, I froze for half a second, then came back online and did what needed to be done. In real crises I can function. The pressure gives me focus.

The trouble begins later. When the noise dies down. When things should feel calm. That is when anxiety arrives. Not in the moment of impact, but in the silence after. You expect peace, and instead your chest tightens, your breathing shortens, and your thoughts circle the same track until exhaustion sets in.

For years I assumed that was just part of me. Static in the background. Something you live with. Eventually I started to notice patterns. They were obvious once I looked for them, but they hid in plain sight because I had never put them on paper. In my professional life we never let events pass without an after action review. What worked. What failed. Where the cracks showed up. You walk the timeline backward until cause and effect come into focus. One day I treated my anxiety the same way. When it showed up, I walked it back. Where was I. What had just happened. What was I avoiding. What did the last few hours have in common. The fog thinned. My anxiety was not coming from threats at all. It was coming from unfinished business. Avoided conversations. Loose ends. Promises I had not kept.

Responsibility I had not carried to completion. The kind of problems you cannot shoot, run, or fight your way through.

That was the first real shift. Anxiety was not noise. It was a signal. Not always fair and not always accurate, but still a signal. Treat it like static and you miss what it is trying to show you. Treat it like information and it starts to make sense.

Once I learned to name it, I stopped running from the things that triggered me and moved toward them. Flying used to rattle me. It did not own me, but it lingered in the background of every trip. So I learned to fly. Not because I wanted to be a pilot. I wanted the fear gone. Once I understood the machine and sat in the left seat with my hands on the controls, the fear evaporated. It did not fade over months. It was gone the moment familiarity replaced mystery.

Water worked the same way. Deep, open water used to unsettle me. Not a pool and not a short swim. The vast kind of water that does not negotiate. If something goes wrong, you are at its mercy. That fear lived longer than I wanted it to, so I confronted it. I started the process of my scuba certification. Not for a thrill or a story. I wanted to strip the fear of its leverage. Once I immersed myself with a competent instructor and felt my breath move steady under pressure, the anxiety dissolved.

The principle is simple. What you avoid, you teach your brain to fear. What you approach, you teach your brain to accept. I did not need a study to convince me. My life was proof. Still, the science aligns with it. Repeated, voluntary contact with a trigger allows the nervous system to recategorize it. Avoidance keeps the brain in a danger loop. Contact gives it a chance to revise the threat.

I began to treat anxiety as a practice rather than a problem. First I caught it in real time and gave it a name precise enough to work with. Not a general sense that something felt off, but the exact thing I had not done. Then I moved toward that thing in the smallest version available. Five honest minutes on the phone. A short drive to the airport to sit at a gate without flying. A quiet hour with my phone in another room. After contact, I rewrote the story while it was fresh. I recorded what I had expected, what actually happened, and what I would do next time. That order matters. Identification. Naming. Exposure. Reframing. The work is simple when you do it, and impossible when you keep it in your head.

This does not erase anxiety, but it changes the balance. It takes power away from what feels bigger than you. When you move toward it, you stop being prey. Anxiety rarely survives direct contact. Ignore it and it grows. Try to outthink it and it shifts shape. Face it with intention and the power dynamic flips.

I have not solved anxiety and do not expect to. I have learned its behavior. It hides in patterns we do not question and thrives in the spaces we avoid. It loses ground when we name it, study it, and step into it on purpose. That is enough. I am not interested in managing anxiety just well enough to function. I want to dismantle it. If I am going to live with it, I want to strip it of mystery and remove its leverage. Identification and exposure have done more for me than anything else.

If you recognize the same undercurrent, the tension that shows up in quiet rooms when nothing is wrong, test this for yourself. Not to prove anything and not to cure yourself. Test it to see what happens when you stop backing away. Start by catching it when it shows up and writing down where you are, who is involved, and what your body is doing. Treat that note like data. Be specific when you name it. Anxiety tied to a phrase like something feels off will not help you act. Anxiety tied to I have not returned that call or I owe a decision I keep delaying can be handled. Then take the smallest step toward contact. If you fear the conversation, schedule five minutes and ask for a clear outcome. If you fear the water, get in a shallow pool and stay until your breath slows. If you fear the silence, sit with it long enough to hear your first excuse appear and then disappear. Afterward, write what happened and decide what you will do next. Small steps that you repeat will beat dramatic vows every time.

None of this requires heroics. It asks for honesty and consistency. Your body will try to pull you back into old reactions. Tight chest. Shallow breath. Jaw clenched. Fingers seeking a distraction. That is an alarm, not an identity. Answer the alarm with something simple that you can repeat. Slow your breathing until your exhale is longer than your inhale. Fix your eyes on a stable point across the room. Sit or stand in a posture you would use if you were calm and then let your physiology catch up. Decide on one next action and take it. The mind calms faster when the body moves in the direction of responsibility.

I have seen the same pattern inside teams. Groups carry anxiety like individuals do. It shows up as meetings that say nothing, passive agreements that hide confusion, and constant urgency about the wrong things. The cure is the same. Identify where the spikes happen, name the real cause, make contact with the smallest version of the process until the friction reveals itself, and then rewrite the standard in plain language. When after action conversations are routine, truth becomes information instead of drama. Teams settle because the work is clear.

Anxiety taught me something else that I did not expect. It taught me what I care about. Fear exaggerates priorities. It points at unfinished duties and unspoken truths. It reminds you who you would rather not disappoint and what you would rather not lose. When I paid attention to where anxiety showed up, I learned where I was most likely to back away from responsibility. That is not a failure.

That is a map.

The metaphor that opened this book keeps returning to me here. The arrowhead in your hand did not begin sharp. It was shaped by pressure applied in the right places until flakes fell away and an edge appeared. Anxiety is part of that process. Each honest contact with what you avoid is a controlled strike. You remove one thin slice of fear and then another and then another. The piece does not transform in a single blow. It turns useful through patient work that looks small from the outside and feels significant only after you step back and notice you are not the same person who began.

Courage is not the absence of anxiety. Courage is the decision to move through it. The same energy that once paralyzed you can become fuel when you direct it toward action. Fear and focus live close together. The more often you make contact with the thing you avoid, the more you discover that most of your anxiety was anticipation, not reality.

In the end I keep returning to the same simple sequence. Catch it. Name it. Make contact. Rewrite the story with what actually happened. Do it again tomorrow. Do it when you are tired. Do it when no one is watching. Over time the quiet moments start to feel like they should. Not empty and loud, but steady. That steadiness is not a gift. It is an edge you earn, one small strike at a time.

PROCRASTINATION

It's ironic this took me a while to write. Not because I lacked time, but because I kept second-guessing it. Would it resonate? Would it matter? Was it worth shaping half-formed thoughts into something clear? Eventually I reached the point where I said, enough. Put it down. That moment when you stop overthinking and act is where procrastination loses its grip.

Most people think procrastination is laziness. That is the story we are told: if you put things off, you must not care enough, you lack discipline, you are weak. Teachers repeat it. Managers enforce it. Self-help slogans polish it. Hear that long enough and you stop questioning the story.

But laziness is not the truth, or at least not the whole truth.

I spent years in places where hesitation had real consequences. Rules were strict, timelines mattered, and deviation was not tolerated. In settings like that, procrastination becomes something else. It is not laziness. It is rebellion. When every part of your life feels controlled, delay is the one lever you can pull. You cannot control much, but you can control when. That small pause feels like freedom.

That is when I began to see procrastination differently. Not as a flaw, but as a signal. A quiet protest that says, I do not want to be doing this, at least not right now.

The problem is that this instinct does not stay put. It follows you home. It bleeds into everything. You start putting off conversations, projects, and responsibilities, not because you are idle, but because something in you feels cornered. Procrastination becomes escape.

That is why the usual advice about procrastination, make lists, manage your time better, hold yourself accountable, often falls flat. None of it works if you ignore the root. Procrastination is not about the task. It is about your relationship to control.

That realization changes everything.

When you remember that you are free, procrastination loosens. You do not have to go to work tomorrow. You do not have to return that call. You do not have to pay your bills. There will be consequences, yes, but the point is that you always have a choice. Once you remember that, the weight shifts. You are no longer acting because you are forced to. You are acting because you choose to.

That simple reframing is powerful. The moment you stop treating obligations as sentences handed down by an invisible authority, you gain leverage. Instead of resenting what needs to be done, you own it. A task becomes a decision, not a punishment.

Seneca wrote, "It is not that we have a short time to live, but that we waste a lot of it." The line is overused, but sit with it and it becomes hard to ignore. Wasting time is not just scrolling or watching TV. It is drifting through days in resentment, convinced you are shackled to obligations you never chose. That is the real waste.

Most of what you think you have to do is not fixed. It is negotiable. You can walk away from more than you realize. You can say no. You can let some things fall. You can leave. Knowing that frees you to take ownership of what remains.

Seen through that lens, procrastination stops being an enemy and becomes a compass. It points to the places where you feel least in control. The conversations you are avoiding. The work you resent. The responsibilities that do not align with who you are or what you want. Procrastination is feedback. It is your system saying, something is off.

That does not mean you give in to it. It means you study it. Walk it back the way you would walk back anxiety. What exactly am I putting off? Why? Fear of failure? Fear of judgment? Resentment toward who is asking? Or is it a task that does not matter and should not be on my plate at all?

Clarity changes how you engage. If the task matters, face it. Strip it of power by stepping in on purpose. If it does not matter, cut it loose. If it is fear, move toward it until it no longer owns you.

Procrastination thrives in vagueness. The less defined the task, the easier it is to delay. The cure is not hacks. It is specificity. Do not say, "I need to get in shape." Say, "At 7 a.m., pick up this weight ten times." Do not say, "I need to call my dad." Say, "At lunch, dial his number and stay on the line." The smaller and clearer the action, the less oxygen procrastination has to burn.

Sometimes the act itself is enough. Sometimes it builds momentum. Other times it simply clears space. Either way, you are out of limbo. You took ownership.

Approaching procrastination this way reveals patterns. The tasks I delay most are not always the hardest. They are the ones I resent. The ones I never believed in. The ones I accepted out of guilt, habit, or pressure. That is worth noticing. If you spend your life pushing off what you never wanted, the issue is not procrastination. It is alignment.

That is the deeper question procrastination forces: What am I giving my time to? Who am I giving it to? Is this what I want to carry?

Answers will not arrive overnight, but asking breaks the cycle. Procrastination is no longer just delay. It becomes direction.

The more I study it, the more I see procrastination not as

weakness, but as honesty. Your body telling you what your mind refuses to admit. Ignore it and it will keep whispering. Confront it and it will give you clarity.

The way out is simple, not easy. Recognize that you are free. Remember you can walk away from almost anything. Decide, with intention, what you will do, and do it. Not because you are forced, but because you chose it.

That choice, repeated daily, kills procrastination at the root.

It is not about tricks. It is not about white-knuckling a to-do list. It is about freedom and ownership. It is about remembering that your time is yours, and wasting it on resentment is the worst waste there is.

So stop waiting. Stop drifting. Stop treating procrastination like a curse. Pay attention to it. Let it show you where you have been living without agency. Then reclaim it.

You are not stuck. You never were.

You have one life. Do not waste it in delay. Do not waste it in resentment. Choose. Act. Move forward.

It does not have to be dramatic. It does not have to be perfect. It has to be yours.

WHEN IT COUNTS, SKILLS MATTER

You begin by learning how the pieces move.

The first time you feel real pressure, talk is useless. The room narrows. Your hands either know what to do, or they do not. This is where people like to invoke mindset, as if a strong attitude can replace practice. It cannot. You do not think your way through a task your body has never done. You perform what you have trained. That is why skills come first. Mindset has a place, but it is not the floor you stand on. It is the filter that keeps your effort aimed the right way once you have something real to run through it.

I have heard people say mindset is everything. It sounds sharp. It travels well in conversation. It gives people identity without asking for sweat. The truth is simpler. Mindset matters because intent matters, but intent without ability is a promise you cannot keep. If a person walks in with a broken or malicious frame, they are dangerous no matter how many repetitions they can show. If a person walks in with a clear frame and empty hands, they still cannot help when it counts. Orientation decides whether you point in the right direction. Skill decides whether you arrive.

The goal is not to have the right opinions about preparedness. The goal is to be useful when it counts. That means when something happens, you know what to do and you can do it. Not in theory. In contact with the world. You cannot apply a tourniquet if you have never handled one. You cannot read terrain under stress if a map still feels like a foreign language. You will not keep your head when a radio fails if you have never worked comms outside a calm room. Capability is a body of work. It is not something you earn by talking about it or by telling yourself you will rise to the occasion. No one rises. You fall to the level of your training and your standards.

A friend of mine named Jake once summed it up with a simple line. You do not open a chess match with strategy. You start by learning how the pieces move. No one begins with grandmaster lines. First you learn the board. Preparedness works the same way. Until you understand your tools, your environment, and your body, you are not in the game. You are watching from the rail. The people on the board are moving while you tell yourself stories about how you would move if you were there.

Hard skills come first because they are accessible. You do not need a war zone to learn basic trauma care. You do not need a badge to dry practice and master a reload safely. You do not need a wilderness course to navigate with a compass. You do not need a tower to pass clear information on a handheld radio. These skills are inexpensive, healthy to train, and available to anyone who will put in the work. They ask for movement, problem solving, and time under pressure. In the process they build the steady head people like to call mindset. The sequence is clear. Capability first. Orientation strengthens it. Not the other way around.

There is a real relief in this. Skill work is honest. A timer does not flatter you. A compass does not care about your self image. A bandage will not secure itself because you wanted it to. The feedback is immediate and clean. Either you can do the task to a standard, or you cannot yet. That is not a reason to feel small. That is a reason to feel grounded. When the world is full of soft signals, skill delivers hard answers. You see your gap. You close it.

Picture a simple night at home. Power goes out in a storm. Your house drops into quiet. The first instinct for many people is to reach for a phone and hope an app answers the problem. The capable person moves. Lights are staged where they said they would be. Batteries are fresh because they set a small schedule and kept it. There is water ready. There is a routine. The household calms down because someone knows what to do and does it without performance. There is nothing dramatic here. There is only preparation paid for with ordinary attention. That is the kind of life this chapter points toward.

What does it look like to build that life. Start by keeping the sequence clean. Orientation at the front as a filter, then skills as the foundation, then mindset as the stabilizer that keeps performance level when you are pulled into stress. You can feel this order in your body. When you know how to stop bleeding and your hands have learned the steps, your mind gets quieter in a crisis because it has something to lean on. When you can read your map and compass and have walked a few routes, you do not panic if your device dies. When you have passed clear traffic on a radio while moving, a small failure in gear is an annoyance, not a threat. Confidence stops being a costume. It becomes the voice your body uses when it knows the work is real.

The work is not exotic. It is ordinary practice stacked day after day. Learn to stop bleeding. Learn land navigation. Learn basic radio communication. Learn to move your body through space with control. Learn to handle your tools safely. Then repeat. There is a rhythm to this and a loop that holds it together. After each session you capture what happened, what worked, what failed, and what you will change next time. Write it down. Keep it short and honest. Return to your notes before you train again. That is how small mistakes turn into improvements instead of habits.

If lists are the only way you keep yourself moving, you can write them. If you prefer prose, keep it in prose. What matters is that you reflect, because reflection is how you cash the lesson. There is no reason to romanticize that step. It takes five minutes, and it keeps you from inventing stories about your performance. When you skip it, you drift into vague training where ten minutes of clean work gets lost inside an hour of motion. When you keep it, you turn small gains into standards.

Capability needs proof. Talk is cheap, and the point is not to sound capable. The point is to be able to help when the room turns. Build small checks into your life so there is no confusion about whether you can do the basic tasks. From your actual carry position, get a tourniquet on your own thigh in under thirty seconds with clothing on. Wrap a pressure dressing on a forearm in under sixty seconds and finish with a clean, secure wrap that does not unravel. Plan a short route on mixed ground, walk it, and land within one hundred meters of each point while logging your pace count on flat ground and on hills. Program three channels on a handheld, call a partner, and pass a location and a status in two short transmissions with batteries that are not about to die. At night, find and stage a primary light, a secondary light, and spare cells in under twenty seconds without fishing through drawers. None of these checks are complicated. They are simple proofs that your practice connects to reality.

Once you have the basics running, widen your circle. Add stress in small doses. Turn simple reps into scenarios that nudge your heart rate and your attention. Apply a tourniquet after a short burst of movement so you have to control your breathing while your fingers work. Read your map at the trailhead, then leave the easy path on purpose and use terrain association to find your way, knowing you can always return to the last known point. Pass radio traffic while you and a partner have to move around a building or along a line of trees. None of this is theatrical. The goal is not to pretend you are someone else. The goal is to become yourself under a little load.

People often ask how much they should train if they want to be ready in a real sense. The honest answer is that something is always better than nothing, and a little bit of honest work five days a week beats a heroic day followed by long gaps. If you want a frame for a month without turning it into a program, set aside half an hour most days. In the first week, keep it simple. Practice tourniquet application ten times with a rest between reps so each one is clean. Sit with a paper map and a compass and orient them on your kitchen table. Walk outside and count your paces on flat ground until you know your number for one hundred meters. In the second week, add radio work and movement. Label your handheld, program it, and run a short check with a partner. Walk your house at night with safe hands, learn your angles, and stage your lights. In the third week, bring small amounts of stress. Do a few bodyweight movements, then run one medical rep. Spend an evening with lights off and power off, and move your family through the house on purpose so no one is surprised if it happens for real. In the fourth week, tighten everything. Put a timer on your reps, write your results, and decide what three changes will make next month cleaner. None of this asks for a gym or a range or a special trip. It asks for attention and repetition.

There are traps here. Be careful with gear chasing. Buying tools is not training. You can tie purchases to checks. When you pass a standard with your current setup and your notes show a real limit, upgrade on purpose. Be careful with information hoarding. Watching other people do work can trick your brain into feeling like you did it too. You did not. Read a skill, then get up and try it. Be careful with vague sessions. If you write everything down in heroic language but nothing in your life changes, you are using words to avoid work. The fix is boring. Set a timer. Pick one task. Do it cleanly. Then add one more task. The loop will keep you honest if you let it.

A steady mind is earned the same way a steady hand is. Not from motivational lines or loud talk. From exposure. From handling small problems while your pulse is up. From making tiny fixes under pressure until calm becomes familiar. After a month of small work you will not feel invincible. You will feel steadier. Little things will stop rattling you. You will move with more purpose. Your head will be quieter under load because your hands have something to do and know how to do it. That is mindset earned by output. It is not a theory. It is a body of work.

There will be days you do not want to train. Those days are important. Not because you have to grind yourself into the ground, but because keeping a small promise when you are tired teaches you who you are. Most people wait for motivation as if it were weather. They move when the feeling shows up and stand still when it does not. If you flip that, everything changes. You move, and the feeling follows. You train for ten minutes and the resistance gets quieter. You keep the loop running and, slowly, the person you are when it counts begins to feel like the same person you are when nothing is happening.

Some people read this and say they do not want to live on alert. They want peace. That is fair. But capability is not the enemy of peace. It is the spine of it. The person who knows how to act can relax more fully because they are not performing relax. They are not pretending everything will always work. They have met small versions of problems and can meet larger ones with the same posture. That way of living spreads to other rooms of your life. Finances get steadier because you keep simple records and stop kidding yourself about the numbers. Relationships get calmer because you say what you mean and listen for what is actually being said. Work gets simpler because you set a standard, hold it, and correct gently before drift becomes failure. Skill practice is not a hobby. It is a class that repeats under every part of your day.

Do not confuse being busy with becoming capable. You can fill every evening with motion and never move forward. The measure is whether you can do the thing when it matters. When a kid falls and bleeds more than they ever have and looks to you without words, do your hands move. When a friend calls from the side of the road and does not know where they are, can you ask the right questions and get them home. When power goes down in your building and people start to crowd and worry, can you pass a few calm words and help them see the next step. Capability is visible to the people around you even if they cannot name it. It feels like presence. It is made in private.

It helps to choose a few standards you will protect without ceremony. You will keep your lights staged. You will carry bandaging and a tourniquet if your local rules allow it, and you will know your gear well enough to use it without thinking. You will keep a real map where you live and where you travel, and you will know how to read it. You will keep a handheld charged and you will not turn it into a toy. You will move your body because it is the only tool you will ever own that cannot be replaced. None of this needs to be posted online. Quiet, private standards often hold better than public vows.

As your base grows, your posture will change in ways other people can feel. You will stop arguing about ideas that never touch your life. You will stop performing intensity about problems you are not responsible for. You will pull your attention toward what you can reach and make better. That is not small thinking. That is responsible thinking. The person who can stabilize a room is more useful than the person who can win an argument in one.

There is a point where the work begins to feed itself. You notice a weakness, you address it, and the fix gives you a little more calm. That calm frees up energy. You spend that energy learning something else or refining something old. You get better at noticing drift early. You speak up at the first sign of it, to yourself and to others. You stop letting tiny cracks turn into large repairs. That is the quiet payoff of skill work. Life stops surprising you in the same ways. New problems arrive, but you meet them with an old posture. That posture is the real treasure. Calm. Clear. Decisive without being reckless. Attentive without being nervous.

You will fail sometimes. You will miss a rep, forget a step, or make a poor call and see it in the results. The temptation is to protect your image and tell yourself a kind story. Resist that. You do not need a kind story. You need a clear one. Tell yourself what happened and what is yours to fix. Do not punish yourself. Adjust. People waste years stuck at the level of almost capable because they protect a role instead of building a skill. There is no role to protect here. There is only a standard that either holds or does not yet. When you treat it that way, your progress speeds up because you are no longer spending energy on a mask.

If you train long enough, you will meet people who treat this kind of work like costume. They will learn the language and buy the equipment and skip the part where your hands get rough from small practice. Their interest will move from one idea to another without ever becoming depth. Do not chase them. Do not judge them either. Focus on your house. Keep your promises. Keep your notes. Keep your loop. Over time the difference becomes obvious in the way your life feels on ordinary days.

When something goes wrong, no one will ask about your mindset. They will look for a person who can help. Can you steady the room. Can you advance the solution. The person who skipped the basics becomes extra weight. The person who kept simple standards becomes a hinge that lets the door move. The good news is you do not need permission to be that person. You can start today. The work is physical. It is cheap. It is available. It sits inside your control. If you do it, the calm you want will arrive as a byproduct. If you skip it, you can still talk about calm, but it will not be yours when you need it most.

In the end, everything here is about love as much as it is about skill. The people you care about deserve someone who can help carry the heavy end of the day. A calm hand in a crisis is a gift. A map that makes sense when everything feels lost is a gift. A voice that can cut through noise with one clear sentence is a gift. You do not buy those gifts. You build them. You earn them with repetition and with a clear sequence that keeps you honest.

Start with orientation. Decide who you are and what you are willing to be responsible for. Then build skills until your hands can speak for you. Let mindset grow in the soil of that work until it becomes the quiet music that plays in your chest when the room narrows. There is no deadline on this. There is no finish line. There is only the life you are building. If you want it to hold when the weather turns, build it on something harder than talk.

Mindset will come. You will earn it.

MAKE CAPABLE COOL AGAIN

We used to admire the kind of person who could figure things out. Someone who could stay calm, assess a situation, and take action without falling apart. That didn't just mean knowing how to survive a disaster, it meant being the one who could fix the broken sink, navigate a problem at work, jump a dead car battery, or talk their way through a complicated moment without looking around for someone else to take the lead.

Being capable wasn't a gimmick. It wasn't about being flashy or putting on some tough-guy persona. It was about knowing that if something went wrong, you could handle it. It was about being competent, and it was something people used to take pride in.

Now it feels like that has completely flipped. More and more, I see people not only lacking basic skills, but actually bragging about it. Like it's funny or impressive to not know how to do anything for yourself. The phrase "I've got a guy for that" has become a punchline people deliver with pride, as if outsourcing every single task is some kind of high-status move. But it's not. If you've made the decision to outsource something because your time is better spent elsewhere, that's one thing. But if you literally don't know how to do it at all and you're proud of that, that's a completely different conversation.

There's also a growing detachment from reality that's made this worse. A lot of people walk through life thinking nothing bad will ever happen to them. They assume that systems will work, professionals will always show up, and they'll never be the one who has to respond in a critical moment. That kind of dissociative thinking makes people fragile. It leaves them unprepared when real-world problems show up, and problems show up more often than most people care to admit.

Being capable isn't just about having the right skill set, it's about knowing how to apply it under pressure, keeping yourself and others calm, thinking clearly in chaos, and adapting to constantly changing variables. That kind of composure is a dying trait, and the only reason I keep writing about it is because it still matters in every aspect of life, whether you're at home, on the road, at work, or in an actual emergency. The ability to stay grounded and effective when everyone else is spinning their wheels isn't just useful. It changes outcomes.

I think a lot about old-school James Bond. Not the Hollywood nonsense or the gadgets. I'm talking about the version of Bond who could blend in, stay composed under stress, drive any vehicle, think tactically, and work a problem from any angle. Sure, he had gear and backup, but that's not what made him effective. What made him effective was that he could solve problems in real time. He didn't fall apart. He didn't look for someone else to take charge. He trusted himself, and he earned that trust by becoming someone who had done the work ahead of time. He was cool because he was capable.

Compare that to what we see now. I was at a cigar bar in Boca Raton a while back, talking with a close friend about how hard it is to properly hang a commercial-grade door. It's not a basic handyman job. It takes precision, an understanding of the structure, weight distribution, and a good eye for details most people miss. My friend, Domsky, who has since passed away, taught me how to do it years ago. He was one of those people who made hard things look easy, and talking about the process was a way of paying respect to that.

While we were talking, a guy at the bar overheard and decided to chime in with, "Why would you even want to do that? I've got a guy for that," and then he chuckled like that was some kind of flex. But I just shook my head. If he had said something like, "I used to do that stuff, but now I pay someone because I value my time differently," I would've respected that. That's a conscious decision made from a place of understanding. But being proud that you have no idea how to do something important or useful, and laughing about it like you're above it, that's exactly the mindset I'm talking about. That's the rot.

What people don't realize is that this kind of attitude has consequences. When you don't know how to do anything for yourself, you become dependent. And when you're dependent, you're vulnerable. It's not just about inconvenience, it's about giving up control of your life and placing all your confidence in the hope that someone else will always be available to fix your problems for you. But what happens when that guy doesn't answer the phone? What happens when you're on your own and something breaks, or goes sideways, or turns into a situation where you don't have time to wait around?

The people who hold it together in moments like that aren't superheroes. They're not geniuses. They're just competent. They've built skills over time, failed at things, figured it out, paid attention, and kept their hands in the work. They've put in the reps, and now when something happens, they can say, "I got this," and actually mean it.

That kind of person doesn't have to be the best at everything. They just need to be familiar enough with a broad range of things that they're useful in most situations. The term I've used before is a capable generalist. Someone who doesn't panic when the lights go out. Someone who knows how to ask the right questions, start the right tasks, and carry their weight without turning it into a production.

When we normalize incompetence, we make everything worse. We make our homes more fragile, our workplaces more dependent, and our society less resilient. We stop innovating because fewer people understand how things actually work. We stop building things ourselves, so we stop valuing the people who can. And then one day, we look around and realize we're all stuck waiting for someone else to show up with the skills we never bothered to learn.

This isn't about being macho or trying to prove something. It's about getting serious about the world we live in. It's about deciding that it's not okay to be completely helpless. It's about bringing back a baseline level of competence and self-reliance that used to be normal. No one is saying you have to go it alone or be some self-contained survival machine. But you should be able to contribute. You should be able to take care of yourself and the people around you when it matters.

Convenience is fine. But if you can't function without it, that's a problem.

So if you're looking for a place to start, start with this. Aim to be the kind of person who can figure things out. Someone who knows what to do when something breaks, or doesn't work, or goes wrong. Someone who can be useful in a crisis, calm in a conversation, and deliberate in how they approach a challenge. Because when the pressure hits, the person everyone wants nearby is the one who knows how to act. The one who doesn't flinch. The one who's been there before.

It's time we stop pretending helplessness is charming. It's not. Let's bring back the person who takes pride in knowing, doing, building, fixing, solving, and carrying the weight when it needs to be carried. Let's make capable cool again.

YOU ARE THE APEX

We hunted mammoths for sport. Not for survival. For sport. We ran gazelles to death, barefoot, powered by nothing but patience, grit, and legs that didn't quit. We didn't just survive the Ice Age, we looked around at the glaciers, shrugged, and got to work. Every time humans entered a new ecosystem, something massive and terrifying vanished. Giant ground sloths, saber-toothed cats, woolly rhinos. Extinct. We didn't coexist. We cleared house.

We are the only species to dominate every biome on Earth. We tamed fire, built tools, wore the skins of our prey, and turned bones into weapons. We took caves, turned them into homes, then into fortresses, then into cities, then into empires. We crossed oceans in wooden boats using the stars for GPS. And when we ran out of land to conquer, we went to the moon just to say we did.

We didn't grow claws or fangs. So we made them. Spears, bows, swords, guns, missiles. We engineered machines that could fly, dive, and explode on command. We turned wolves into pets, horses into tanks, apex predators into accessories. There are full-grown tigers living in Las Vegas next to guys named Gary who sell time-shares. No other species does that. Just humans.

Nature threw everything it had at us. Plagues. Parasites. Famines. Viruses. We ate it all. Sometimes it almost broke us. But we adapted, healed, and came back smarter. We invented sanitation, figured out antibiotics, mapped our own genome, and now we're rewriting it like a rough draft. We didn't just survive nature's wrath. We learned to edit it.

And not only do we know what an atom is, we split it. We cracked the building blocks of the universe and weaponized them. We built machines that can erase entire cities. We gave ourselves the ability to end everything, not by accident, but because we figured out how. That is not normal apex predator behavior. That's human behavior.

You can find this main character everywhere. Arctic. Jungle. Mountain. Ocean. Doesn't matter. If humans show up, everything changes. We adapt. We dominate. We survive. And we do it better than anything that's ever existed.

There has never been anything like us. Evolution didn't make a better animal. It made us.

We didn't lose our apex status. We just stopped acting like it.

Not everywhere. There are still parts of the world where survival is non-negotiable. Where clean water, secure food, and physical safety are daily concerns. Where people fight for every inch of life. But in the modern first-world, most people haven't faced real hardship in years. Some, not ever.

We built comfort so well that it started working against us. The same minds that planned hunts and tracked seasons now panic over notifications and scheduling conflicts. The body that evolved to endure heat, cold, hunger, and miles of movement now needs ergonomic chairs, apps to count steps, and daily reminders to drink water.

This isn't about men or women. It's both. The weight of disconnection from effort, from struggle, from the satisfaction of doing hard things, is crushing everyone. Men were built to provide and protect. Women were built to endure and nurture. Both were built to overcome. And both have been sold a lie that ease equals happiness.

Most people are medicated. Overstimulated. Exhausted by ease. We've replaced real achievement with performative versions of it. We cosplay strength online and then call for help when the Wi-Fi goes down. We've hacked life to the point where carrying your own groceries is seen as exceptional. Self-reliance is now a subculture. That should tell you something.

This is what happens when apex predators forget they're apex. Thousands of years of evolutionary pressure can't be silenced by convenience. That edge we earned gets dull when it's not used.

Comfort is killing us. Slowly, quietly, with a smile. And most people will never feel it happening.

You can't kill evolution with comfort. The instincts are still there, buried under modern life. The drive to move, to build, to defend, to overcome. That part of you that wants something harder, something real. It's not a midlife crisis. It's biology, tapping the glass.

The solution isn't to reject comfort. It's to earn it. To build a life where ease is the reward, not the default. You were made to struggle, and then adapt. That doesn't mean you need to sleep in the woods and eat bugs. It means you need to stop outsourcing your entire life.

Cook your own meals. Carry heavy things. Wake up early. Get cold. Get hot. Take care of your body like it's the only tool you'll ever have, because it is.

Learn something difficult. Fix something broken. When my sink exploded at 11 p.m., I figured it out. Not because I knew how, but because no one else was coming. That feeling, the moment you solve a real problem without a safety net, rewires something in you.

Start a skill stack that makes you more useful and less dependent. You don't have to become a blacksmith or a backcountry hunter, but you should know how to handle yourself when systems fail. Learn basic medical skills. Navigate without a GPS. Understand how to defend yourself. Make fire. Purify water. Patch a wound. Stay calm when things fall apart.

Give your brain what it evolved for. Terrain. Threat.

Planning. Pattern recognition. Get off the treadmill and walk uneven ground. Turn off the algorithm and read something that challenges you. Get bored. Get focused. Let the silence stretch long enough for your instincts to wake up.

This isn't about pretending to live in the woods. It's about being dangerous to the right things. Dangerous to weakness. Dangerous to complacency. Not for the sake of violence, but for the return of control.

You are not meant to feel lost in a world that hands you everything. That feeling isn't failure. It's a warning.

Feed the beast what it wants. Capability. Struggle. Growth. Do hard things on purpose. And watch how fast everything changes.

You don't need permission to take control. You don't need a certificate or some curated routine to begin. What you need is a quiet moment of clarity. A decision to stop coasting and start building. A choice to remember what you are and live like it.

You were made from generations of people who endured war, famine, disaster, and heartbreak and kept going. You carry their resilience in your blood. You are the product of struggle. The product of pressure. And if that part of you feels underfed, it's because modern life starves it.

So feed it.

Get uncomfortable on purpose. Learn to run without headphones. Carry your groceries without a cart. Fix something instead of replacing it. Cook your meals from scratch. Learn the basics of first aid, navigation, and self-defense. Turn down the noise long enough to hear what your instincts have been screaming.

And when things get hard, remember this. Those

moments of difficulty are the ones you'll look back on with pride. The miserable hikes. The nights without power. The time everything went sideways and you figured it out anyway. That's the good stuff. That's what turns into stories. Into lessons. Into the kind of quiet confidence that can't be faked.

None of this is about pretending to live in a cave. It's about regaining agency. It's about earning peace instead of expecting it. And it's about modeling something better for the people around you. Capability spreads. Confidence spreads. Strength, when earned, lifts everything it touches.

The truth is simple. You are the apex predator. Not by muscle. Not by speed. By will. By thought. By the ability to adapt, overcome, and improve. That is your edge. It always has been.

So sharpen it.

You are the apex. Start acting like it.

THE CRUCIBLE OF FAILURE

Failure has shaped me more than anything else in my life. It stripped away illusions faster than time, humbled me harder than success ever could, and carved the edges I carry now. Every collapse, every misstep, every wrong call was a debt collected, and every payment became tuition in the only school that matters.

Most people spend their lives running from failure. They treat it as if it is poison, something to avoid at all costs. But the truth is harsher. Failure is the crucible. It is the fire that tests what you are made of and burns away what cannot endure. Without it, you remain soft, untested; Smooth enough to look intact, but too fragile to survive real pressure.

When I think about the moments that defined me, almost none of them were clean victories. They were setbacks, losses, and mistakes that forced me to grow sharper than I wanted to be. Success confirmed the skills I already had. Failure revealed the ones I did not. And it is in that gap, the uncomfortable space, where you are exposed that growth actually happens.

So I do not see failure as an enemy anymore. I see it as the toll-keeper. If you want to cross into anything worth having, you pay with failure first.

Failure does not arrive gently. It burns, it humiliates, it strips you bare in a way that comfort never will. That sting is why most people avoid it. They would rather live in the illusion of safety than stand in the fire long enough to be changed by it.

But that sting is the whole point. The fire exposes. It shows you exactly where you were weak, unprepared, or dishonest with yourself. You can lie to others, you can even lie to yourself for a while, but failure will not let you. When the bottom drops out, there is no performance left. Only truth.

I have felt that fire more times than I can count. Deals I thought were secure collapsing overnight. Plans I poured everything into turning to ash. Moments where I realized too late that I was not ready, and there was no rewinding the clock. In those moments, you do not feel enlightened. You feel small. Ashamed. Broken open in a way that no one claps for.

And yet, every one of those flames left me sharper. The fire did not care about my pride, my excuses, or my intentions. It only cared about results. It burned off the excess, left behind scars, and forced me to rebuild. That is the crucible. The paradox is that the very thing people spend their lives avoiding is the only thing strong enough to forge them into something real.

Failure is not subtle. It does not leave you guessing. It arrives like a hammer and leaves you staring at what is broken. That is why it teaches faster than success. Success comforts you. It convinces you that you have arrived, that your method works, that you can relax. Failure does not allow that illusion. It makes you examine every decision, every detail, every assumption you carried into the moment.

I have learned more from the nights I walked away empty-handed than from the victories that padded my pride. When something collapses, you do not get the luxury of pretending. You have to look straight at the gap between who you thought you were and who you actually are. That sting, that humiliation, is the sharpening stone.

Failure strips away arrogance. It humbles you in a way that no advice or lecture ever could. It makes you admit that you did not know as much as you thought, that you were not as sharp as you believed, that the margin for error was thinner than you wanted to admit. Success will never teach you that. Success feeds pride. Failure cuts it down and makes room for clarity.

It also forces adaptability. Once you have been burned, you stop assuming the fire will not touch you again. You start preparing differently. You check the details twice. You learn to improvise when the plan goes sideways. You stop expecting a smooth road and build the frame of someone who can handle rough ground. Failure conditions you to move quicker, adjust faster, and recover stronger.

And there is something else. Failure makes you honest. Not just with the world, but with yourself. In the moment when everything falls apart, there is no room for excuses. You can blame circumstances, you can point outward, but the fire still burns in your chest. Deep down, you know where you fell short. That honesty is painful, but it is the only path forward.

That is the true lesson. Success confirms what you already are. Failure shows you what you need to become. And it is through those lessons, repeated and often brutal, that you earn your edges.

One of the hardest lessons I ever learned about failure did not come from combat or training. It came from business. I joined a friend in what I thought was a solid venture. I trusted him. I believed we were building something together.

Then, without warning, I was forced out. Ninety days later I found out the truth. The business had been quietly positioned for sale the entire time. The paperwork, the negotiations, the big payout, all had been in motion long before I was pushed aside. By the time I discovered it, the deal was done. The kind of money that could have set me up for life was on the table, and I was not even in the room.

The failure was not just the betrayal. It was mine as well. I had trusted a handshake where I should have demanded a signature. I had mistaken friendship for partnership, assuming loyalty where I should have insisted on clarity. And I paid the price.

That sting has never left me. Not because of the money, though that loss was real, but because it forced me to confront how naive I had been. I had allowed myself to believe that intent was enough, that trust alone could hold the weight of a business venture. That was a failure of judgment, and it carved a permanent edge into how I operate.

Today, I put everything in writing. I separate personal trust from professional structure. I do not confuse good intentions with guarantees. That failure taught me a lesson I could not have learned any other way: when the stakes are high, clarity is not optional.

The strange thing about failure is that it feels like the end in the moment, but in reality, it is the beginning. The sting convinces you that you are finished, that you have ruined your chances, that you will not recover. But every time I have been burned, every time I thought I was done, the opposite turned out to be true. Those failures became the foundation for the next chapter.

The paradox is this: the people who work hardest to avoid failure end up the weakest when it finds them. They spend their lives staying safe, protecting an image of being untouched, trying to look flawless. And when the strike finally lands, they shatter. Fragility masquerading as strength.

The ones who are forged differently are the ones who walk into the fire and accept the cost. They fail, they burn, they rebuild, and they come out sharper than before. Every scar becomes a kind of armor, not to keep them from failing again, but to remind them that they have survived it before and will survive it again.

Failure is unavoidable. You can spend your whole life dodging it, but it will still find you. The difference is whether it breaks you or builds you. The people who spend years avoiding failure are shocked by its weight when it arrives. The ones who face it willingly are already conditioned to carry it.

That is the paradox. Failure looks like loss, but it is actually leverage. It takes everything from you in the moment, and then, if you let it, it hands you back something more valuable: resilience, clarity, and an edge that cannot be faked.

Failure is not a detour on the road to success. It is the road. Every scar, every humiliation, every collapse is a toll you pay to move forward. The only question is whether you let those moments harden into excuses, or whether you carry them as sharpened edges.

I have lost money, trust, and opportunities I thought I would never get back. At the time, each one felt like the end. But standing here now, I see them differently. They were beginnings. They stripped me of illusions I did not know I was carrying and forced me to rebuild on solid ground.

The truth is, failure never stops hurting. It is not supposed to. The sting is what makes the lesson stick. But if you treat it like a teacher instead of a sentence, the same fire that once burned you will forge you into something stronger.

I think of a line from Samuel Beckett: "Ever tried. Ever failed. No matter. Try again. Fail again. Fail better." That is the standard. Not perfection. Not untouched victory. But the willingness to fail better each time, to sharpen yourself through the fire, and to come out of the crucible with edges you could not have earned any other way.

Because in the end, success is just failure refined.

THE RAZOR'S EDGE OF SIMPLICITY

We live in a time where the dramatic explanation is often preferred over the honest one. Every major event seems to spawn theories of hidden actors, shadowy agendas, or complex schemes too clever for the average person to grasp. It isn't only online conspiracy communities that fall into this trap. We all do it in smaller ways, imagining that someone slighted us for reasons deeper than they did, assuming a business decision was orchestrated with grand design rather than simple incompetence, or believing that success must be the result of some secret system instead of consistent effort. The temptation is always to reach for the story with layers because it feels more interesting, more validating, more worthy of attention.

Occam's Razor stands in direct opposition to that tendency. It is the principle that the explanation requiring the fewest assumptions is usually the right one. No drama, no intrigue, just the discipline of trimming away what doesn't hold up. It doesn't guarantee truth, but it does something more valuable: it creates a starting point. It forces you to look at what is plainly in front of you before letting your mind wander into speculation. That makes it one of the most practical philosophical tools available.

The real value of this way of thinking isn't in winning arguments or debunking elaborate theories, it's in how it shapes your own decision-making. When you train yourself to start with the most direct explanation, you save yourself from wasted energy, bad assumptions, and poor judgments. You see people more clearly, you evaluate risks more honestly, and you respond to problems with a steadier hand. Occam's Razor isn't just a principle, it's a personal edge. The ability to resist needless complexity is as rare as it is valuable, and it gives clarity in a world that constantly tries to cloud it.

When people chase conspiracies, it isn't always because they believe them. Sometimes it's because a complicated story feels safer than a simple truth. If a single man with a rifle can alter history, then life is fragile in a way that's hard to accept. It's easier to imagine hidden networks and masterminds pulling strings than to face the idea that chaos and incompetence often drive events. Complexity becomes a kind of comfort, a shield against the randomness of the world.

But it isn't only conspiracy theorists who fall into this. You see it in boardrooms when people would rather commission a market study than admit they missed calls and dropped follow-ups. You see it in relationships when silence is read as betrayal instead of fatigue. You see it in your own mind at 2 a.m., building a story about why things went wrong when the reality is just that you made a bad choice. The longer the story gets, the further you drift from the truth.

Occam's Razor doesn't make life more pleasant. If anything, it strips away the comfort that complexity provides. It leaves you with the blunt answer, and the blunt answer is often uncomfortable. Failure usually comes down to not being ready. Conflict often starts because you said the wrong thing. Success is often the result of nothing more glamorous than working harder for longer. There's no poetry in that, but there's clarity—and clarity is what keeps you from repeating mistakes.

In high-risk environments, simplicity isn't philosophy, it's survival. The man who complicates the problem with imagined variables usually ends up frozen. The one who cuts straight to the most likely cause and acts on it has the advantage. When a weapon goes down, you don't start theorizing about why—carbon build-up, a faulty spring, poor maintenance—you clear it and get the gun back in the fight. When a vehicle stops running in hostile territory, you don't sit around speculating about complex electrical faults, you check fuel, spark, and air first. The fastest path back to action is usually the simplest, and the man who can discipline himself to follow that path earns time. Time is the one resource you never get back.

The same thing plays out in planning. Teams sometimes fall into the trap of building elaborate explanations for failure. They imagine sabotage, hidden politics, or forces working against them. Sometimes that's true, but most of the time the answer is right in front of them: someone didn't prepare, someone didn't communicate, someone didn't execute. Leaders who can strip away noise and focus on the direct causes move faster and hit harder. They don't allow themselves the luxury of complexity until the facts demand it.

Occam's Razor, applied here, becomes a weapon against hesitation. Complexity is paralyzing. It gives you endless excuses to delay action while you gather more information, while you wait for clarity that may never come. The discipline to start with the simple answer, act on it, and then expand only if it proves wrong—that's what keeps you moving. In a fight, in business, or in life, motion itself is often the edge.

Clarity is contagious. When a leader sees through a problem and communicates it in simple, undeniable terms, everyone under them sharpens. They stop wasting energy on theories and start focusing on execution. That's the difference between a team that reacts and one that dithers. Complexity slows groups down, while simplicity pushes them forward.

Most people don't lose their way in combat or in business, they lose it in the small, private spaces where no one is watching. Occam's Razor cuts just as sharply there. The reason you're not where you want to be isn't usually hidden or mysterious. It's not that fate singled you out, or that some invisible system is working against you. More often it's that you avoided the hard work, chose comfort, or let yourself drift when you should have pushed. The blunt answer stings, so people search for a complicated one.

It shows up in relationships too. Silence from a friend doesn't always mean betrayal. Distance from a partner doesn't always mean a hidden agenda. The simplest explanation—that they're tired, or busy, or preoccupied—often gets ignored because we'd rather create a story that confirms our fears. We make life heavier than it needs to be by layering it with assumptions.

Facing the plain truth requires humility. It forces you to take responsibility where you'd rather assign blame. It asks you to accept that life is not a mystery novel where every thread connects to some grand revelation. Sometimes the reality is blunt and boring. You failed because you didn't prepare. You lost because you weren't good enough that day. You're alone because you didn't do the work of showing up.

This doesn't make life easier. It makes it harder in the short term and clearer in the long term. And clarity, when it's earned, gives you a kind of freedom. It lets you stop wasting energy on imagined layers and start doing the work that actually matters.

The truth rarely flatters. It strips away the comfort of theories and the safety of excuses. It leaves you with the answer sitting in front of you, waiting for you to stop avoiding it. That's all Occam's Razor really is—the refusal to decorate failure, to soften weakness, to disguise responsibility.

But the man who can cut straight to the simplest explanation, accept it, and move from there is the man who cannot be stalled. He doesn't waste time weaving stories that protect his ego. He doesn't chase complexity for its own sake. He deals with what is, and he acts.

That discipline is rare. Most people reach for noise when faced with clarity, because noise is easier to live with. But if you want an edge, you can't afford it. The man who can live with the simple, unpolished truth—about the world, about others, about himself—carries a sharpness the rest will never know.

WHAT YOU PROTECT, REVEALS WHO YOU ARE.

There's a certain kind of man who doesn't need to be told what his role is. He feels it in his chest before it reaches his mind. He doesn't wait for permission, doesn't look for recognition. He just knows. His job is to protect what matters.

That sense of responsibility doesn't come from pride or fear. It comes from something older. Something deeper. A bond forged in presence. The kind that makes you instinctively take the outside seat. The kind that makes you sleep light when others need rest. The kind that makes you carry more than your share because you know they can't.

It isn't a performance, and it isn't posturing. It's the quiet promise that whatever crosses that line, you'll be the one who answers for it. When something you care about is in the blast radius, your body moves before your mind does. Not because you are reckless, but because the decision was made a long time ago.

That instinct is ancient. And no matter how far removed we are from the world that shaped it, it hasn't left. You feel it when something doesn't sit right. You sense it when you walk through the door and take in the room without thinking. You see it when someone looks at you and relaxes, even if they don't know why.

You were built to protect. That is not toxic. It is not outdated. It is clarity.

This isn't about being a hero. It is about being capable. About taking ownership of your space and the people in it. About living in a way that says, if something happens, you will be the one who handles it. Calm. Ready. Without hesitation.

Because at some point, if you are fortunate, you will find something or someone that matters more than your own comfort. And in that moment, you will understand a truth that doesn't need to be explained. The most honest expression of love is not what you say. It is what you protect.

That is the foundation. That is where it starts. Everything else builds from there.

It doesn't happen all at once. There's no single moment where you feel yourself slipping. No flashing sign that something essential is fading. Instead, it is quiet. Subtle. A slow, steady drift from who you were meant to be.

Maybe it starts with comfort. A little more ease than you intended. Maybe it begins when responsibility gets lighter, or when you realize no one is depending on you the way they used to. Or maybe it's something deeper. A steady erosion from the inside out. The world no longer asks you to be dangerous for the right reasons, and so you stop preparing for anything real.

At first, you stay busy. You keep up the routine. You still show up. But underneath it all, you feel the absence of weight. The lack of urgency. You lose the reason behind the discipline. The structure remains, but the substance starts to thin.

When that happens, most men don't spiral. They substitute.

They look for something to fill the gap. Something to stand behind. Something to fight about. That is when you start seeing men throw themselves into causes or conflicts they are not actually connected to. They become experts in political debates that never touch their homes.

They care more about the outcome of a game than the condition of their household. They argue fiercely over world events, ideology, and cultural issues that make them feel purposeful, even when they bear no responsibility for the outcomes.

It is not wrong to care. There is nothing wrong with having strong opinions. But when all your intensity is poured into things that never require you to follow through, it becomes a distraction. A performance of conviction without the consequence of accountability. Over time, it becomes easier to stay there. It asks less of you. It lets you feel engaged without being required to be present.

What is missing is something real to protect. Something close enough to matter. Something heavy enough to sharpen you.

When you are not anchored by that, you start to soften around the edges. Not in a physical sense, but in the way you move through the world. You stop thinking clearly. You react more. You avoid the hard things because you are no longer practicing how to meet them.

You become tired, not from work, but from floating.

Men are not meant to float. When we have nothing to carry, we lose our frame. We become overstimulated, overinvolved, and undercommitted. We burn energy without direction. We make noise but leave no mark. And slowly, we forget what it felt like to be grounded in something that actually needed us.

You do not need to solve it all overnight. But if you feel unsteady, unfocused, or more irritable than usual, ask yourself a simple question.

When was the last time you truly protected something?

Not from a distance. Not in theory. Something close. Something real. Something you were willing to suffer for.

If you cannot answer that, it does not mean you have failed. It just means it is time to stop drifting.
Sometimes it happens all at once. Other times it builds slowly. But eventually, something real pulls you back.

It might be the birth of a child, when suddenly every decision you make echoes forward into someone else's future. It could be finding the kind of love that steadies you, that raises the standard for how you carry yourself. Maybe it's a parent growing older and starting to lean on you in ways they never had to before. Or a sibling starting a new chapter, or bringing life into the world, and you feel something shift in your chest that wasn't there before.

Whatever form it takes, the result is the same. Your attention narrows. Your posture changes. You stop moving aimlessly and start making decisions with intention. With weight. With meaning.

You are no longer reacting to the world around you. You are responding to something close. Something that needs you to be steady. Something worth carrying.

You begin thinking in terms of consequence. You make choices with clarity. You guard your time more carefully. You hold yourself to a higher standard, not out of pride, but because you know someone else might pay for the moments where you fall short. That kind of pressure does not break you. It focuses you.

And it is not just about protection in the physical sense. It is about structure. About stability. About making sure the things that matter stay upright. You become more deliberate with your presence, more intentional in your preparation, more thoughtful in your habits. You start training not just for strength, but for endurance. For reliability. You sort out your finances, not for comfort, but because unpredictability is no longer acceptable. You think longer-term. You plan for storms, not because you are afraid, but because it is your job to be ready.

This is where direction comes back. You are not perfect, but you are present. You still stumble, but now you get back up for a reason.

There is peace in that. Not the soft kind that comes from avoiding struggle, but the deep, earned kind that comes from knowing you are exactly where you should be. You are needed, and you are useful, and your actions matter.

You begin to speak differently. You stop chasing validation. You stop wasting energy on things that do not move the needle. You learn to let go of what does not serve the mission.

The shift is quiet. It is not a transformation others always notice, but it changes everything. Because when a man reconnects with what he is meant to protect, his life takes shape again. He stops drifting. He starts building.

And once you feel that weight return, you do not want to let it go.

Most people hear the word protection and think of violence. A threat, a response, a physical act. While that is part of it, it is a narrow view. Protection is not always loud. In fact, the strongest forms usually are not.

True protection shows up long before anything goes wrong. It lives in preparation. In foresight. In the way you walk through your life with people in mind other than yourself.

It is easy to say you would die for someone. But would you live for them? Would you stay consistent when it is hard? Would you make the small, quiet choices that no one thanks you for, but that keep things from falling apart?

That is protection.

It is found in how you manage your money. In how you hold the line on standards. In how you speak when tempers rise. It is in whether you have a plan, not just for yourself, but for the people who depend on you. It is in being predictable, in a good way. Steady hands. Clear words. A calm presence when things get loud.

It is walking into the house after a long day and not bringing your frustration with you. It is taking care of your health so someone else does not have to later. It is noticing the details. Remembering the things that matter. Showing up without being asked.

Protection can be physical, but more often, it is structural. It is about what you build around the people you care about. Boundaries. Margin. Security. Routine. Things that make them feel grounded, even if they never see the effort behind it.

And it is not about being perfect. It is not about doing everything yourself. It is about being aware of your role and stepping into it with purpose. Some days you will carry more. Some days you will fall short. But the difference is you do not disappear. You show up again. You recalibrate. You keep your eyes on what matters.

This kind of protection is not reactive. It is proactive. It is thoughtful. It is earned.

And people can feel it.

They may not say anything. They may not even realize why they feel more calm, more safe, more stable around you. But they do. Because your presence is not just physical. It is layered. It is intentional. It is made of decisions you have already made, and work you have already done.

That is what it means to live as a protector. Not just to be ready for the fight, but to make sure the people you care about do not have to live in a constant state of tension. To carry a burden that lets others breathe a little easier.

Protection is not something you talk about.

It is something they feel.

At some point, you have to ask the question.

What do you protect?

Not what you care about. Not what you post about. Not what you feel strongly about when the conversation turns serious. But what, in your life, is actually safer because you are in it?

What have you built a wall around? What have you chosen to stand for, consistently, without applause?

Because the truth is, you are always protecting something. It might be your comfort. It might be your pride. It might be your reputation. But unless you are intentional about it, you might end up guarding the wrong things.

There are men who will throw themselves into debates about the state of the world, who will argue politics with strangers, who will spend hours each day defending abstract ideas online. But ask them how things are at home, how their wife is doing, how often they call their father, how long it has been since they checked in on their kids' headspace, and they come up quiet.

It is not because they do not care. It is because they have not set a standard.

Protection is not passive. It does not happen just because you love someone or believe in something. It happens when you decide to make their wellbeing part of your responsibility. When you stop waiting to be asked. When you draw the line and say this is mine to keep watch over.

And that line does not have to be big. You do not have to lead armies or carry the world. But you do need to know where your post is. You need to know what falls under your care, and you need to take that seriously.

That could mean being the kind of father who does not miss. The kind of partner who sees more than what is said. The kind of brother who checks in even when it is uncomfortable. The kind of man who does not just show up when things fall apart, but lives in a way that keeps them from falling apart in the first place.

This is not about shame. It is about clarity.

Because you cannot live with purpose if you do not know what you are protecting. And you cannot protect anything if you do not take ownership of it first.

So ask yourself.

What do I stand in front of?

What do I carry, even when no one sees it?

What in my life has my fingerprints on it, not because I touched it, but because I held it together?

Set your standard there.

And live like it matters.

NOTES ON LEADERSHIP

I didn't set out to write a rulebook on leadership. I started writing these notes down because I needed them for myself. I was frustrated... wasting time, energy, and money trying to fix problems that kept showing up in the people around me, only to realize I hadn't led them the right way in the first place. And when you keep ending up in the same situation, eventually you have to stop pointing outward and start looking in the mirror.

Leading others starts with leading yourself. That's where all of this began for me. If I'm being honest, I've always been one of the hardest people to lead. I don't take direction well unless it makes sense. I don't respond to hierarchy or credentials. I need logic, clarity, and competence before I'll buy in. That's just how I'm wired. And if I'm that difficult to lead, then maybe figuring out how to lead someone like me was the best place to start.

Over the years, I've ended up in leadership positions, some in environments where the cost of bad decisions is immediate, and others in business, where the consequences are slower but just as painful. These days, I'm the one people look to for answers. I run teams. I advise companies. I build systems. And leadership is a central part of everything I do.

What follows isn't theory. These are real principles I use. Some were learned the hard way. Some I've had to relearn more than once. I wrote them down because I needed a reference point for myself. And if they help someone else sharpen their edge or avoid a few costly mistakes, even better.

I. SET EXPECTATIONS SO CLEARLY THEY CAN'T BE MISUNDERSTOOD

One of the fastest ways to lose a team is to be vague about what you expect. If you want accountability, you need clarity. You don't build that by writing a job description or giving a motivational speech. You build it by telling someone exactly what they're responsible for, what success looks like, and what the consequences are if they fall short. Then you make sure they understand it.

That includes what you don't care about. Most leaders focus only on what they want, but people remember it when you give them space on the things that aren't mission critical. If you don't care when they show up, as long as the deliverables are done, say that. If you don't care about dress code, or email formatting, or sitting in a chair for eight hours, make it known. The clearer you are about what matters and what doesn't, the more energy your team can put into the work that counts.

Assumptions are where leadership fails. If you never took the time to explain the baseline, you don't get to act surprised when it's not met. And if your standard only lives in your head, it's not a standard—it's a setup for failure.

II. ALWAYS GIVE THE WHY

People need a reason. Even when they act like they don't. If you skip the why, they'll make one up, and it probably won't be helpful.

Giving the why creates direction. It gives meaning to what might otherwise feel like busywork. It keeps your people from asking the same quiet questions over and over. Why are we doing this? Why now? Why this way? Most of the time, they won't ask you directly. They'll just nod, then go back to their desk and second guess the task, the plan, and you.

You don't have to give a speech every time you delegate. But you do need to give enough context that the person understands this isn't arbitrary. Even a sentence makes a difference. "We're doing this because it eliminates two hours of wasted effort every week." That's all it takes to anchor a task to a purpose.

It also builds trust. Explaining the why shows that you respect the people you're leading. It says you've thought it through and that they deserve to be looped in. You get better results, fewer delays, and less friction when people know what they're working toward.

III. DON'T ASK PEOPLE TO DO SOMETHING YOU WOULDN'T DO YOURSELF

You can't lead from a distance. You have to understand what you're asking for. That doesn't mean you have to be better at it than your team, but you do need to have done it, be willing to do it, or at the very least, know what it takes to do it right.

There are times when you bring in people smarter than you in a certain area. That's fine. But you still need to be able to speak their language and guide the outcome. If you're completely hands-off and have no idea what they're doing, you're not leading them. You're just hoping it works out.

If I expect someone to carry weight, I've carried it first. I've done the grunt work. I've stayed late. I've walked into the tough meetings. That's not about pride—it's about credibility. If someone sees that you've done the thing you're asking them to do, they'll respect the ask. If they know you wouldn't hesitate to do it again, they'll take it seriously.

Leadership means knowing the job and not being above the work. If you lose that, you lose the team.

IV. GIVE PEOPLE THE TOOLS TO WIN

You can't expect results from people you didn't equip. If you want performance, you have to invest in it. That means giving people the right tools, the right training, and enough room to actually use them.

This shows up everywhere. Whether it's giving someone the software they need to move faster, the access they need to make decisions, or the time they need to train before being thrown into the deep end. You are responsible for setting the conditions. When your team knows you've set them up to win, they work harder. Not because you told them to, but because you've shown them it matters.

It also reinforces your credibility. Even if you haven't done the exact job they're doing, you've done something close enough to understand the pain points. You've dealt with pressure, timelines, client expectations, and the constant threat of things falling apart. That's the kind of experience that helps you anticipate what people need before they ask for it.

Don't make people beg for what they need. Don't hand off responsibility and then walk away. If they're not set up to succeed, and you're the one who put them there, that's your failure. Not theirs.

V. NORMALIZE AFTER ACTION REPORTS

Everything gets an after action. Good outcome, bad outcome, doesn't matter. You run it every time so people expect it. That way, when things go wrong, it's not a witch hunt. And when things go right, you don't miss the chance to lock in what worked.

It's not just about learning. It's about giving your team a safe space to talk. Everyone wants to vent. Everyone wants to say what they really thought about how it went. If you don't give them a way to do that constructively, they'll find other ways—usually behind your back, or not at all.

Make the after action the place for that. Let people air their complaints, but only if they do it with the intent to improve something. No aimless bitching. No blaming without owning. Reward the people who bring up real problems and tie them to real solutions. That's how you build a team that trusts each other enough to tell the truth.

When you make debriefs a standard, people stop being defensive. They start expecting feedback, and they start giving it to each other. That's where real growth happens.

VI. DON'T CONFUSE SILENCE WITH AGREEMENT

Just because someone doesn't say anything doesn't mean they're aligned. Silence is cheap. Most people would rather nod and get out of the room than raise a hand and slow things down. But that kind of silence is dangerous, because it creates false confidence.

You can't let unspoken doubt slide. You have to pull it out. Ask for pushback. Check for clarity. Make sure people are really tracking. Because when they're not, and they go off in the wrong direction, you're going to pay for it later.

This doesn't mean you babysit. It means you read the room and confirm alignment. You should be able to say, "Tell me what you heard," without making it feel like a quiz. You're not testing them. You're verifying communication.

The goal is understanding, not agreement. And you won't get either if you treat silence like a green light.

VII. ADDRESS PROBLEMS EARLY, NOT EVENTUALLY

When something's off, deal with it. Don't wait. Don't rationalize it. Don't hope it self-corrects. It won't.

Small problems become big ones fast. A missed deadline

turns into a pattern. A half-effort task becomes a baseline. If you don't address it right away, you're telling the rest of the team that the standard is flexible. And once people realize they can slip without consequence, they start testing how far they can go.

Dealing with things early keeps them small. It doesn't have to be a dramatic intervention. It can be a five-minute check-in, a quick course correction, a private call to ask what's going on. The point is to keep your hands on the wheel and steer before you're in the ditch.

You're not doing anyone a favor by ignoring issues. You're just letting them grow into something harder to fix.

VIII. PROTECT THE STANDARD, NOT THE PERSON

It's easy to let high performers get away with things. Or to overlook small issues because you like someone. But every time you do that, you weaken the standard.

You can't lead based on who you like. You have to lead based on what's right. If someone is great at their job but toxic to the team, that needs to be handled. If someone consistently cuts corners but never gets checked because they're seen as "critical," you're building a fragile system around one person.

Protect the standard first. Everyone else is watching. If they see you enforcing it fairly, they'll respect you. If they see you bending the rules, they'll start bending them too.

Leadership isn't about avoiding hard conversations. It's about setting the tone. The moment the standard only applies to some people, it stops being a standard. It becomes a suggestion.

LEADERSHIP IS EARNED EVERY DAY

Leadership isn't about having authority. It's about what you do with it. You don't get to call yourself a leader just because your name is on the door or because people report to you. That part's easy. What's hard is showing up consistently, setting the tone, and making sure everyone around you knows what's expected and why it matters.

You're responsible for the standard. You're responsible for the direction. And you're responsible for making sure people are equipped to do the job well. If there's confusion, it's on you. If there's dysfunction, you own that too. You don't get to distance yourself from the outcomes once you've taken the seat. That's the trade. You carry the weight, or you don't lead.

This isn't about being perfect. It's about being accountable. It's about paying attention to the things that matter and correcting course when you drift. The best leaders I've worked with, the ones I've followed without hesitation, didn't need to remind anyone who they were. They just did the work, held the line, and made sure the people around them had what they needed to win.

If you're going to lead, do it with purpose. Don't delegate it to hope. Don't hide behind a title. Don't wait for things to go wrong to start paying attention. The team will follow your example long before they follow your instructions. Make sure it's one worth following.

THE PARADOX OF COMMUNICATION

We're born knowing how to communicate. There's no instruction, no vocabulary, and no real understanding of language, but the message still gets across. A newborn cries, and the world responds. Before we ever speak a single word, we already know how to express need, discomfort, frustration, and fear. It's instinctive. It's natural. It just happens.

But as we grow, something shifts. We learn words. We learn tone. We learn how to persuade and argue and refine. In theory, we should be getting better. In reality, most of us get worse. We hesitate. We bury what we mean. We sharpen our words into weapons or dull them until they mean nothing. The more important the message, the harder it seems to deliver.

That is the paradox.

The most natural skill we have is also one of the most difficult to do well. And nothing else matters without it. Every relationship, every team, every success or failure, comes down to this one thing.

I've watched entire projects collapse because of communication. Not because people weren't talented, not because they weren't motivated, but because no one said what they meant or listened to what was said. Silence became agreement. Sarcasm replaced clarity. People assumed understanding where there was none. By the time anyone noticed, trust was already gone.

I've felt it in my personal life too. Arguments that weren't really about the surface issue at all, but about the words left unsaid months before. Friendships that drifted because neither side admitted something was wrong. Even love that fell apart, not because of a lack of care, but because the care wasn't communicated clearly enough to be believed.

The cost is always the same. Distance.

When I started reading what the philosophers had to say, I wanted a solution. Something clean. A principle I could apply and never get this wrong again. That never came. Wittgenstein warned that words aren't mirrors of reality. The more we try to sound precise, the less clear we become. Kierkegaard said that self-awareness breeds fear, and fear makes us indirect. Buber argued that real connection requires presence, not performance, and most of us settle for performance.

They were right. I've seen it in myself. Times where I tried to sound sharp and ended up unclear. Times where I held back out of fear, where the risk of being seen felt heavier than the risk of being misunderstood. Times where I went into a conversation like a performance instead of a connection, trying to win instead of listen.

But philosophy alone wasn't enough. I needed to see where this showed up in the real world.

On one end of the spectrum, I know people who can't be serious. Every time the conversation drifts toward something meaningful, they use humor as a shield. They're good at it—sharp, witty, always ready with a line. But the price of that defense is distance. You never get past a certain point.

On the other end, I know people who treat every conversation like an attack. No matter how carefully you phrase it, they hear judgment. They brace for impact before you've even spoken. And once that wall goes up, you can't get through. What should have been a simple exchange turns into a battle no one meant to fight.

Neither person is bad. Both are protecting themselves. But the cost is the same: connection never happens.

And I'm not above it. I lean toward the opposite problem. I speak directly, often too directly. That works in some places. It gets things done. But in others, it cuts deeper than I intend. I've said things that were technically true but landed in ways that cost more than they solved. I've had to learn that being right isn't the same as being effective.

So what do you do with all this?

For me, it comes down to a few simple shifts. Clarity beats cleverness. Presence beats performance. Silence doesn't equal agreement. And communication is never finished—it's practiced. Like any other skill, if you stop working on it, it decays.

That's why I've started paying more attention. Did what I say land the way I meant it? Did I listen long enough to actually hear, or was I just waiting to speak? Did I make the hard thing clear, or did I try to soften it until it lost meaning? These are questions worth asking.

Because at the end of the day, communication isn't about style. It's about connection. We start life knowing how to cry when we need something. Then we spend the rest of it learning how to hide, how to protect, how to complicate. Getting better at communication isn't about learning something new. It's about remembering something old.

Most of the problems I've seen in life—teams breaking, relationships ending, opportunities missed—didn't fall apart because people lacked ability or intent. They fell apart because someone didn't say what they meant, or someone else didn't hear what was actually said.

Communication is both the simplest thing we know and the hardest thing to do well. That paradox isn't going away. But the closer we can get—closer to clarity, closer to presence, closer to honesty—the stronger everything else becomes.

And maybe that's the real edge. To strip away the layers, to stop performing, and to simply mean what you say.

THE PITFALL TEST

Opportunity is seductive. It whispers about what could be gained, about the victories waiting on the other side if only you say yes. Most people fall for that first impression. They picture the rewards, they sell themselves on the upside, and only later, sometimes too late, they discover the hidden costs that were there from the start. I learned the hard way that the shine of possibility can blind you to the cracks underneath, and that once you are dazzled by potential, you stop noticing the floor moving under your feet.

That is why I began running every decision through what I call the pitfall test. It is not about paranoia. It is about discipline and posture. Instead of asking what is the best that could happen, I ask where this collapses on me. I ask where the catch is, where the trap is, which angle I am not seeing. It reverses the usual process. Rather than building a brief for why the thing will work, I try to break it before it gets the chance to break me. I slow the frame down, subtract the excitement, and make myself hold the idea under harsher light than the world will, because the world will test it with no warning and with no concern for what I hoped would be true.

The pitfall test is a mindset, but it is also a method. You strip the gloss off the opportunity and walk around it with blunt questions. What assumptions am I smuggling in without proof. What if the people involved are not acting in good faith. What happens if the variables do not line up in my favor. How much of the upside depends on timing, and how much depends on me. By digging into those questions early, I avoid falling in love with the illusion of certainty. Ideas do not need my affection; they need pressure.

That pressure does not kill opportunity. It hardens it. If the idea survives the test, it has already proven itself against forces worse than polite skepticism. If it fails, I have saved myself time, money, and reputation. The pitfall test is about balance. It is the willingness to look past the surface, the refusal to be lulled by the promise of what could be, and the awareness that sometimes the strongest move is to walk away before the ground gives out. Saying no is not the opposite of ambition. Often it is the proof that you are still in charge of it.

Think of the test as a deliberate pause between excitement and commitment. It is the habit of stepping back far enough to look for weaknesses you would prefer not to see. Instead of rushing toward gain, you stop and ask where the soil is soft, where the cracks are hidden, and how the plan would unravel if two or three things tilt against you at the same time. The supplier pulls out, the loan reprices, the partner hesitates, a regulation letter arrives, the weather turns, the key hire quits, the market punishes your timing. If the structure topples under a plausible string of bad luck, you have your answer. If it bends and holds, you have something you can build on.

It works because clarity is built on friction. When you put your own idea under pressure before the world does, you strip away illusion and see what remains. The pitfall test converts enthusiasm into interrogation. In that conversion the weak assumptions announce themselves. What looked clean under a soft light begins to show its hairline fractures. That is good news. You can only fix what you can see, and you can only see what you are willing to name.

More than a tactic, the test is a discipline. It demands honesty when you would rather indulge hope, and restraint when momentum tempts you forward. Discipline does not suffocate opportunity. It protects you from blind spots that turn small bets into large regrets. Most wrecks do not come from one catastrophic error; they come from a stack of unexamined beliefs that finally lean too far in the same direction. The test forces those beliefs into the open where they can be weighed, confirmed, or discarded.

Running the test begins with a change in posture. Instead of asking, Why will this work, you ask, Where could this break. That single shift pulls you out of the role of salesman and into the role of interrogator. In salesman mode you polish the upside, handle objections, and rehearse the pitch until you believe it yourself. In interrogator mode you start digging with the intention of finding something you will not like. If you do not find anything, you keep digging until you are confident you looked in the right places.

The first weak point is usually assumption. Every decision is full of them. You assume people are acting in good faith, that conditions will stay favorable, that your information is complete, that timelines will hold, that costs will stay in range, that attention will not drift, that luck will not run out at the worst possible moment. These are fragile supports. The test begins by dragging them into the open and asking for receipts. Which of these assumptions can I verify today. Which of them can I hedge. Which of them must remain uncertain, and what is my plan if they break against me.

Then you follow the trail of consequences. If this fails, who gains. If this stumbles, where do the costs land. Incentives are the map under the map. They reveal the angles, the unseen fees, the quiet preferences that will govern behavior once the talking stops. A deal that looks balanced on a slide may be completely out of balance in practice, with risk sitting squarely on your shoulders while someone else collects most of the reward. The pitfall test forces that accounting in advance, not after signature.

Finally you imagine the moment when conditions tilt against you, not the best case or even the average case, but the sharp turn you never see coming. The supplier pulls out after a larger customer calls. A partner betrays trust with a small lie that reveals a larger pattern. A variable you cannot control moves at the wrong time. A competitor ships earlier. A dependency fails upstream and slows everything down just as your burn rate peaks. If the idea collapses completely in that scenario, you have just saved yourself. If it flexes but holds, it is stronger than it looked and you have learned where it needs reinforcement.

The pitfall test grew out of experience, not theory. It is the product of years spent learning what happens when trust is misplaced or when excitement outruns judgment. After enough of those lessons, I stopped waiting to be surprised and started asking the blunt question up front: how am I going to get screwed here. It sounds harsh, but it is not bitterness. It is clarity. It reframes disappointment into challenge. My job is to red team my own thinking and to find the angles that would undermine it before anyone else does. Where is the imbalance. Who benefits if this fails. What am I blind to right now because I want this to be true.

Oddly, I like the process. It is problem-solving in its cleanest form. Each flaw I uncover sharpens the decision. When an idea collapses under the pressure of the test, I have saved time and pride. When it holds, it has proven its strength in a way that a good mood never could. The habit keeps me from being reckless, and it still lets me move fast when the upside is real. Confidence earned under pressure travels further than confidence borrowed from a mood.

There is a boundary that matters here. Skepticism protects; cynicism corrodes. The difference is subtle but critical. Skepticism is active. It asks hard questions, digs for weaknesses, and forces you to earn your confidence before you move forward. Cynicism dismisses everything without testing. One sharpens judgment. The other strangles it. The pitfall test lives on the skeptical side of the line. It is not a machine for saying no. It is a filter that helps you say yes with your eyes open.

The hardest salesman to defeat is the one in your own head. You will be the first person to sell yourself on an idea. You will replay the pitch until the holes become background noise. You will smooth out the ugly parts in your mind and inflate the parts that feel like destiny. Every pass will make it harder to hear the doubt that kept you safe the first time you considered the bet. That is why the test is necessary. You have to stop being your own advocate and become your own adversary. You have to pressure test your conviction before anyone else gets the chance to.

A common pattern shows up. You spot a new opportunity and, instead of interrogating it, you begin rehearsing the upside. You think about how much money it could make, how quickly it could move, how it could change your position. By the third or fourth time you have gone over it, you have polished away the doubts. You are no longer testing the idea. You are marketing it to yourself and mistaking the echo for proof.

The way to interrupt that cycle is simple and unglamorous. Write down the failure points. Not the rosy scenarios and not the pitch. Write the three ways this could break you in terms you cannot ignore. Put them on paper where they cannot hide inside your optimism. That act forces the weaknesses into daylight. When you catch yourself running the highlight reel, stop. List the pitfalls, face them directly, and decide what you will do if they appear. That resets the frame from optimism to clarity without killing your drive.

Keep the distinction in sight. Cynicism tells you not to bother. Skepticism tells you to probe deeper. One closes doors by default. The other clarifies which doors are worth walking through and which are painted onto the wall. The pitfall test lives in that second posture, and it keeps you from turning caution into fear. The point is not to avoid risk. The point is to price it accurately and to choose it on purpose.

Most people believe power comes from saying yes, from chasing every glittering chance. Often the opposite is true. Power comes from walking away at the right time, not because you are timid, but because the cost of the upside is wrong for you. The test does not only reveal cracks in the opportunity. It gives you permission to step back before you are standing on broken ground and calling it fate.

Walking away does not mean you were foolish to consider the opportunity. It means you were strong enough to put it under pressure and honest enough to accept what you found. That restraint saves resources, preserves energy, and builds confidence in the decisions you choose to pursue. The opportunities that survive the pitfall test are not guesses anymore. They have already been tempered by scrutiny, which means your resolve will not evaporate when the first hard day arrives.

If you keep practicing, the habit becomes second nature. You stop rushing into commitments and you stop letting excitement lead you blind. Your pace changes. You still move, but you move with clarity. You understand that saying no can be as valuable as saying yes, and that the edge you are trying to keep does not come from taking every chance. It comes from choosing the right ones with clear eyes and a clear bill of materials for the risk you are accepting.

That is the real strength of the pitfall test. It does not dull your drive. It sharpens it. By breaking the illusion early, you protect yourself from expensive lessons, you preserve your focus for the work that matters, and you leave space for the opportunities that truly deserve you. If a decision cannot live through that kind of scrutiny, it does not deserve you yet. If it can, then it has already survived the hardest conversation you will ever have about it, the one where you tell yourself the truth.

FAMILY BY CHOICE

Family is one of the most powerful forces in a person's life, but it is also one of the most misunderstood. For some, the word means belonging, a steady table, a place where you can put your back to the wall without looking over your shoulder. For others, it brings up conflict, guilt, and the memory of people who should have protected them and did not. That alone should make us careful about talking in absolutes. Family can be the best thing you ever have or the first thing that tears you apart.

From the time we are young, we are told that blood makes a claim. Family first. Blood is thicker than water. Never turn your back on your own. These phrases survive because they sound noble, because they hint at a code that could hold a life together. But reality is more complicated. Some people spend years carrying relatives who refuse to carry themselves. Others discover that the most reliable, loyal, and honest bonds they will ever know come from people they are not related to at all. Neither story cancels the other. It only proves that family is defined by behavior, not by slogans.

There are families that sharpen you. A father who shows what discipline looks like when no one is watching. A mother who keeps her word when it costs. A sibling who does not flinch when the room goes quiet and the bill comes due. The lessons do not always arrive wrapped in warmth. Sometimes they come as standards, as lines you are expected to hold without applause. The gift is not comfort. The gift is clarity. Strong families do not remove hardship. They prepare you to meet it with your feet under you.

Family also arrives through circumstance. Bonds forged in conflict, disaster, and shared risk. Men who deployed together. Women who worked the same ER through a winter that would not end. Teams that pulled strangers from collapsed concrete and did not break. These ties are not about convenience. They are built under pressure, when the cost of a mistake is measured in lives, not opinions.

And then there is the circle you build on purpose. Mentors who invest when there is nothing to gain. Friends who stay in the fight after the easy excuses run out. A partner who steadies you when everything else starts to tilt. Blood can begin the story. Choice is what keeps it honest. The people you keep close are the people who have proven they belong there.

Family is not one shape. It shows up in blood, in situation, and in choice. What matters is not what you call it. What matters is whether it is real.

Most of us inherited a script. Family comes first. Keep the peace. Do not air dirty laundry. If you follow that script without thought, you can spend a lifetime paying bills you did not create, apologizing for lines you never crossed, and pretending that title and trust mean the same thing. They do not.

The quiet danger sits inside the word itself. Family sounds like a promise, so people treat it like a guarantee. But not all families are built the same. Some are anchored by earned respect. Others run on secrets and pressure. Enmeshment gets labeled loyalty. Enabling gets labeled love. A relative calls with a demand and you call it a responsibility because saying no feels like betrayal. Meanwhile the person you are protecting never changes, because nothing in their world insists that they must.

I have seen the roles play out. The hero who fixes everything, then burns out in silence. The scapegoat who absorbs blame so the system never has to be honest. The golden child who learns the worst lesson of all, that effort is optional if enough people are afraid to tell you the truth. These are patterns, not destiny. But they thrive when "family" blocks the view of what is actually happening.

There is another cost. Assumption distorts your definition of love. If love means you cannot hold a line, love becomes permission for harm. If love means you cannot speak the truth, love becomes a performance. If love means you must accept whatever behavior walks through your door, love becomes a tool for control. None of that is love. It is fear dressed as loyalty.

Letting go of the assumption does not mean abandoning the people who raised you. It means judging the relationship by what it produces. Do these people help you grow into someone reliable, useful, and honest, or do they keep you small? Do they celebrate your progress, or do they demand that you remain who you were when they were most comfortable? Those questions matter more than any phrase you were handed as a child.

The weight of assumption is real. Carry it long enough and it will bend your life into shapes that do not belong to you. Set it down and you make room for something stronger, a family built on clarity instead of pressure, on presence instead of pretense.

Not every story is a story of damage. There are homes where standards are normal, where people keep their word, where apologies are spoken without a defense attached. Those homes create useful people. They are not perfect. They argue, they miss, they repair. What makes them different is not the absence of conflict. It is the expectation that conflict will be met with honesty and a return to the line.

Think about the small things that add up. A parent who shows up on time, every time. A table where phones are put away because conversation matters. A budget that stays inside its lines because debt is not an option. These habits seem ordinary until you live without them. Then you realize they were a quiet defense against chaos.

A strong family makes you face yourself earlier than you would otherwise. It does not let you outsource your character. It does not treat comfort as a goal. It insists that the private version of you match the public one. It does not flatter. It tells the truth kindly but clearly. Later in life, when the pressure hits, you recognize that tone. You lean into it, even when it feels inconvenient, because you have learned that standards are a form of love.

There is a secondary effect. When you have been sharpened well at home, you become the person others can trust outside of it. You are the one who checks the gear, who reads the contract, who calls back when you say you will. People feel safer around you, not because you are loud, but because you are consistent. That is the mark of a family that did its job.

Honor that. It is rare, and it is worth protecting. It does not require a spotlight. It requires maintenance.

There is another kind of family that is neither born nor selected. It is made by the pressure of a shared burden. You stand beside someone in a moment where the outcome matters and you both feel the weight. After that, something permanent exists between you.

Sometimes it is literal proximity. Soldiers who lived in the same mud, walked the same alleys, stared into the same dark doorways, and learned the same names for fear. Firefighters and medics who cut strangers from metal at three in the morning, then go home and try to sleep with the smell of gasoline in their clothes. Nurses who ran short-staffed nights for months and kept each other upright with coffee and gallows humor. Teammates who kept a small company alive by working through weekends, not for a bonus, but because running out of runway would have cost people their jobs. None of this is theory. Pressure introduces you to people in a way ease cannot.

Sometimes the bond does not come from being there together. It comes from recognition. Two veterans in line at an airport hear the name of a city, a border, a country that did not hold. They nod, and the conversation changes. Abuse survivors hear a detail others would miss and understand. People who have buried someone too young notice the way the room goes quiet in one corner of your eyes. The details differ. The weight is the same. The shorthand forms instantly.

Family by situation is powerful because it strips away performance. You do not need to justify yourself. You do not need to explain why you moved the way you did when the moment came. The other person already knows. Trust is accelerated because the margin for deception was erased by the kind of reality that does not care about your story.

For many people, these ties run deeper than blood. They are not inherited. They are not owed. They are earned by showing up, by staying calm when others spin, by doing the simple, difficult thing for as long as it takes. Time can pass without contact and the bond does not fade. When you finally meet again, you return to the same frequency in a breath.

There is a warning here too. Not every shared hardship should become your identity. Some experiences need distance before they can be named without turning into anchors. But once you have the distance, pay attention to the people who carried the same kind of load and kept their shape. They are rare, and they are worth keeping close.

If blood is what you were born into and circumstance is what you were thrown into, choice is what defines you. The family you build on purpose is the proof of your values. Anyone can inherit a last name. Not everyone can assemble a circle that reflects what they claim to care about.

Family by choice is not a rejection of your relatives. It is a commitment to alignment. You surround yourself with people who move the same direction and who prove, repeatedly, that their word can carry weight. It is not about finding clones of yourself. It is about finding people whose strengths and standards make you better when you are close to them.

You do not drift into the right circle. You decide. You watch what people do when no one is watching. You notice who is willing to be bored while doing the right thing. You test with small trust before you offer large trust. You pay attention to how they talk about people who are not in the room. You look for patterns, not performances. The circle that endures is built from many small confirmations, not one dramatic favor.

The people who belong in this circle will show up without being reminded and leave quietly without a bill for the help. They will not mistake access for leverage. They will not take your wins personally or your losses as proof that you are no longer useful to them. They will correct you privately and defend you publicly. They will not demand to be the only voice, and they will not vanish when you choose differently. In return, you do the same for them.

Over time, this chosen family becomes the house you can carry with you. Jobs change, cities change, seasons change. The circle persists. The conversations shorten because the trust is already paid for. Advice lands faster because it is rooted in shared history. And when life gets loud, you do not need to audition for support. You already know who will answer the call and who you need to be for them.

Family without boundaries becomes a liability. Family with boundaries becomes a force. Lines are not about punishment. They are about keeping love in a shape that does not collapse under its own weight.

Too many people confuse love with permission. They allow

behavior they would never tolerate from a stranger, then call the exhaustion "the cost of caring." They say yes when they mean no, then resent the very people they were trying to help. They keep giving chances without changing terms. Over time, the pattern eats their time, their money, their energy, and their clarity. This is not love. It is fear of loss. The fix is not hardness. The fix is standards.

Start with ownership. Decide what you will carry and what you will not. That includes money, time, and emotional labor. If a relative refuses to own their part, your willingness to over-function will not save them. Make help conditional on effort. Make access conditional on respect. Make repeat appearances conditional on change. Say this plainly once, then live it quietly. Lectures do not set boundaries.

Consequences do.

Protect your yes. A yes means something when your no is real. If you say yes because you fear conflict, you are not kind. You are vague. Vague kindness becomes cruelty fast. People who care about you will adjust to your lines. People who only care about the access you provide will not. That is the point. A boundary is not a wall to keep everyone out. It is a gate that makes clear who can come through and on what terms.

Apply the same standards to chosen family and situational family. Shared hardship does not excuse bad behavior. Proven loyalty in one season does not entitle anyone to your silence in another. The truth spoken early keeps relationships healthy. You can forgive without inviting someone back into a role they have already shown they cannot carry.

At home, this looks like small commitments done exactly. Schedules that are kept. Money that is tracked. Voices that stay calm when tempers want to rise. Sleep that is protected because you do not ask others to pay for your fatigue. Rituals that keep the house steady in the ordinary weeks so it can hold when a hard week arrives. Standards are not cold. They are the structure that allows warmth to survive.

In the field, this looks like clarity under pressure. Everyone knows the plan. Everyone knows their job. After action reviews are normal. Praise is specific. Corrections are clean. The team does not wait for emergencies to practice communication. The standard belongs to everyone, not to a single person whose absence would collapse the whole thing. That same clarity belongs in your closest circle. It does not make love smaller. It makes it repeatable.

Family is not a single category. It can be the people who raised you and set a standard. It can be the people who carried the same weight and earned your trust under pressure. It can be the circle you built on purpose because your values required it. The label matters less than the proof.

Some people earn their place by how they live when no one is watching. Some earn it by staying steady in moments that would have broken others. Some earn it by showing up long after applause and audience are gone. The rest is noise. DNA, sentiment, and obligation mean very little if the behavior does not match.

If you are fortunate, you will know all three kinds of family in one lifetime. Blood you respect. Brothers and sisters born of hardship. A chosen circle that keeps you honest and strong. If you only get one, choose the people who have demonstrated, again and again, that they can be trusted with weight.

Because when everything unnecessary falls away, family is not who you were told to trust. It is who is still there, doing the work, with their hands on the same load as yours.

KNOW YOURSELF FIRST

Marcus Aurelius wrote that nowhere can a man find a quieter or more untroubled retreat than in his own soul. That line has stayed with me because it is not poetry to me. It is a map. If you do not know that retreat, everything you build will shake when the wind picks up.

I have spent long stretches of time alone. Geographically. Emotionally. Professionally. It did not bother me. It helped. There was no one to impress. No performance to keep up. Only space. In that space a person either learns who he is, or he goes searching for someone else to hand him a name. If you choose the second path, you will ask other people to carry a weight that belongs to you. Some will try. None will be able to hold it for long.

Most relationships that break do not explode. They erode. One person begins to lean on the other for peace, identity, or steadiness. At first it feels like closeness. It looks like intimacy. It sounds like trust. Slowly it becomes something else. Expectation. Need. Burden. The other person starts carrying more than their share. They become a wall to hold back your storms and a mirror to hold up your worth. No one can do both for very long.

I have watched strong people fail under this quiet load. A man who wanted a partner but really needed a rescue. A woman who wanted love but really needed a place to store fear she had not faced. They loved each other. They tried. But the bond was built on borrowed strength. When the balance shifted even a little, the whole thing tilted. Not because they were bad or dishonest. Because the work had not been done where it had to be done. Alone.

The Odyssey is not a story about boats. It is a story about a man who cannot come home until he has faced himself.

Odysseus is delayed by storms and monsters and gods, but that is not the heart of it. The heart is that he is not finished yet. He has to be broken down to what is true. Only then can he come back to his life with Penelope and hold it steady. The old world understood this. We have forgotten it. We try to come home early and ask someone else to carry our unfinished parts.

Solitude is not a waiting room. It is a proving ground. When you are alone, your defaults show up. Your excuses lose traction. You hear what you say to yourself when there is no audience to correct or praise you. You notice how much of your day is spent avoiding silence and how fast your hand reaches for a screen to save you from your own thoughts. If you cannot sit with yourself, you will ask a partner to do it for you. They cannot. No one can.

Knowing yourself is not an abstract goal. It is practical. It is the difference between walking into a room and reacting to every strong emotion, or walking in with a frame that holds. It shows up in small ways. In how you speak when you are tired. In whether you can say no without anger. In whether you can let someone you love be upset with you without falling apart or demanding reassurance you have not earned. It shows up in whether you can carry your part of the day without turning your effort into a performance.

There were times in my own life where I leaned too hard on someone else and called it trust. I thought I was being open. I thought I was sharing the load. The truth was simpler and more uncomfortable. I was trying to avoid work I had not done alone. No matter how much they cared, it strained the bond. I was not asking for partnership. I was asking to be held together. That is not love. That is dependency dressed up as intimacy.

A partner can stand beside you. They can help, steady, and remind. They cannot finish the parts you refused to begin. They cannot be your identity. They cannot carry responsibility for your mood, your peace, or your sense of worth. When you push that job onto them, they will either collapse under it or go numb to survive it. Either outcome will feel like betrayal, but the betrayal started before that. It began the day you handed them your center and called it closeness.

There is a reason men used to build rites of passage around solitude, risk, and responsibility. The point was not danger. The point was clarity. A man who has faced himself can be relied on. He does not grab for control when he feels fear. He does not hand off control when he feels tired. He knows the difference between comfort and recovery. He knows when to ask for help and when to carry it. He is not perfect, but he is solid. Solid is enough to build a life on.

You build that solidity by making contact with the parts of you that are easiest to outsource. Your peace. Your direction. Your values. Your work. Start small and specific. Sit in silence for ten minutes before you pick up your phone in the morning. Notice what it feels like to want distraction and not feed it. Write down the three standards you will keep even when no one is there to notice. Keep them for a week. Then a month. Keep them when it is boring. Keep them when you are busy. Keep them when no one thanks you for the effort. That is how you learn which parts of you are real and which parts were performances.

Carry some weight alone on purpose. If you cannot carry money with discipline by yourself, you will not carry it well together. If you cannot carry the basics of your health by yourself, you will turn your body into a debt someone else has to pay. If you cannot carry hard conversations with care by yourself, you will either avoid them or turn them into contests. None of this is dramatic. It is foundation work. Without it, everything looks fine until the first storm.

People often ask how much self-work is enough before you share a life with someone. The answer is not a number. The answer is posture. Are you building a life that can stand without someone else holding it up, or are you waiting for them to become your structure? If your answer is the second, you are not ready. That does not mean you are unlovable. It means you are not finished. There is dignity in admitting that. There is danger in denying it.

There is also a cost to refusing to share any weight. Some people hide inside self-reliance because it feels safer than trust. They pride themselves on never needing anything from anyone. That is not strength either. That is fear dressed as discipline. Knowing yourself first does not mean building a fortress and living alone in it. It means building a frame strong enough to open the door without fear that everything will collapse.

This shows up in work as clearly as it does in love. I have led teams that looked impressive on paper but cracked under pressure because no one owned their part. People waited for direction, then resented it. They asked for responsibility, then avoided it. They wanted the feeling of being trusted without the discipline of becoming trustworthy. It is the same pattern as in relationships. Until a person has decided who they are and what they stand for, they will ask their environment to tell them. The environment will oblige, and then change, and then they will collapse again.

When you know yourself, your yes and your no start to mean something. You do not agree to a project because you are afraid to disappoint. You do not say no because you are afraid to try. You aim your effort where it belongs. You apologize faster when you are wrong because your worth is not hanging on the illusion of being flawless. You praise faster when someone else wins because your identity is not threatened by someone else's strength. This is not theory. This is daily life. This is what it feels like to be with a person who has done their work.

I think often of a man I knew who carried himself with a quiet stability I admired. He had not had an easy life. There were losses, mistakes, and long seasons where progress looked invisible. He did not brag about hardship, and he did not advertise grit. He kept showing up. He decided early that anger would not run his mouth, that fatigue would not lower his standard, and that anxiety would not make his choices. He failed at each of those sometimes. But he had a line and he kept returning to it. People relaxed around him. Not because he made everything light, but because he made nothing chaotic. Presence is a gift. He gave it because he had it to give.

If you want a simple test, here it is. Sit in a quiet room for one hour without a screen. No music. No television. No phone. Think about your life with a pen in your hand. Write the three things you know are yours to fix. Write the three things you know are not yours to carry. If you cannot tell the difference yet, you do not need more noise. You need more silence. Repeat this once a week for a month. Watch what patterns show up. That is you, on paper, without invention. Build from there.

Another test. Ask yourself who suffers the most when you are irresponsible with yourself. If the answer is always the people closest to you, you are not ready to spread your weight. Put it down long enough to be honest. Pick it back up with a standard. Do not announce it. Live it. If someone notices, fine. If they do not, better. Work done without an audience grows deeper roots.

There is a hard truth in all of this. If you do not know yourself first, you will sell yourself cheaply. You will trade peace for attention. You will trade standards for company. You will accept versions of love that keep you from ever becoming the person who could belong in the love you actually want. No one can stop you from making those trades. No one can make them for you either.

So what does it look like to know yourself first in plain language? It looks like taking responsibility for your state before you walk through the door. It looks like having a plan for your money, your time, and your body that aligns with what you say matters. It looks like apologizing without defending. It looks like protecting your sleep, your training, and your focus so you can protect other people when they need you. It looks like saying no to the easy praise of being the loudest person in the room. It looks like knowing what you will not do even when it would be profitable, and what you will do even when it would be costly.

If this sounds severe, it is only because life gets heavy. The people you love deserve someone who can help carry it. You will not always be able to. You will fail. You will be the one who needs rest and grace and help. Knowing yourself first does not remove those days. It prepares you to meet them without making them worse. It keeps you from turning your need into a habit or your fear into a rule for the house.

There is another side to this. When you know yourself, you start to choose people differently. You are less interested in heat and more interested in solidity. You can admire beauty without mistaking it for character. You can enjoy excitement without mistaking it for depth. You can be alone without mistaking it for abandonment. Your standards get clearer, not harsher. Your gratitude gets louder. Your conversations get calmer. Your patience gets longer. Because you are not negotiating your identity every time you sit down with someone you care about.

The work does not end. It does not conclude with a ceremony or a ring or a title. Knowing yourself is not a badge. It is a practice. There will be days when you drift and need to call yourself back. There will be seasons when you are tempted to hand your center to someone else in exchange for relief. You will need to remember that relief is not peace and that borrowed strength always comes due. Steady work beats dramatic vows. You do not have to be perfect. You have to be honest and consistent enough to be trusted.

So before you ask to be understood, know yourself first. Before you ask someone to carry life with you, learn what it feels like to carry it alone. Before you ask for calm, make some. Before you ask for loyalty, be reliable. Before you ask for peace, stop feeding chaos. Do this not because you are trying to earn love, but because love deserves a place to live that will not collapse under it.

When the silence shows up, and it always does, it will tell the truth about you faster than any speech. Be the person who can sit in that silence without reaching for a distraction or a rescuer. Be the person who can breathe there. Build that room in your soul. Walk into it often. Bring back what you find and live by it. That is how a life becomes solid. That is how two lives can stand side by side without becoming a single crutch.

Know yourself first. Then invite someone in.

EARN YOUR GOOSEBUMPS

Goosebumps are an ancient reflex. Technically called piloerection, it's a built-in response triggered by the autonomic nervous system, specifically the sympathetic branch, the same one responsible for fight or flight. When early humans were cold or threatened, tiny muscles called arrector pili would contract, causing the hairs on their skin to stand upright. In animals with fur, this either trapped heat or made them appear larger to predators. For us, with far less body hair, the effect is practically useless.

Or so it seems.

Because even today, this response still activates. Not just from cold or fear, but from music, memory, awe, grief, pride, adrenaline. A national anthem. A war film. A funeral. A mountaintop. The birth of your child. A performance that stirs something primal. The same evolutionary wiring that once signaled survival now fires during moments of deep emotional charge.

So maybe it's not useless at all.

Maybe it's a physical marker of meaning. A reminder that you're not just going through the motions. You're feeling something. You're present. You're alive. And if that's the case, then goosebumps aren't a leftover from the past. They're a compass. A signal worth paying attention to.

Because in a world that numbs, distracts, and sedates us at every turn, the moments that give us goosebumps are rare. And maybe that's exactly why we should chase them.

Some things give me goosebumps every time. The American national anthem. The final movement in Mahler's Titan. There's a weight in those moments I can't explain.

It hits hard and without warning. My skin reacts before my mind does. It's automatic.

Then there are the times it sneaks up on me.

Like when I get on my motorcycle. It doesn't happen on every ride. But once in a while, everything lines up. I let the clutch slip into first, and feel the 1200cc engine come alive. I find that balance between speed, lean, and tension. The road hums under me, the wind tightens around my shoulders, and the bike feels weightless. Just for a second, everything disappears. And I feel it. That rush. That surge. Goosebumps.

Not from fear. Not from cold. From presence.

That feeling reminds me I'm not just passing time. I'm in it. Awake. Alive. And the more it happens, the more I've started to wonder why I don't chase it more often.

Because most people aren't. They wait for those moments to show up instead of going out and finding them. But what if you could? What if you knew how to? What if you learned what gives you that feeling and made it part of your life on purpose?

That's where we're headed next.

Everyone's wired a little differently. What gives me goosebumps might not even register for you. That's the point. This isn't about copying someone else's thrill. It's about figuring out what moves you.

Start paying attention. Not just to the obvious moments, but to the subtle ones. What were you doing the last time you felt your chest tighten in a good way? When did the world fade out for a second and something inside light up? What were the sounds, the smells, the pressure in the air? Who were you with? What was at stake?

These moments are clues.

You don't need to go skydiving or chase some extreme version of life. That's not what this is about. This is about noticing the feeling when it does hit and tracing it back to its source. Maybe it's music. Maybe it's competition. Maybe it's building something, teaching someone, standing up for something that matters, or stepping into the unknown.

The mistake most people make is thinking those moments are random. They're not. They're earned. And once you figure out what causes them, you can start shaping your life around more of it.

That doesn't mean chasing dopamine or becoming a slave to adrenaline. It means building a life with friction, with depth, with sharp edges and meaning. A life that stirs you.

That's how you know you're doing it right.

The more you start paying attention, the more patterns start to show up.

It took me a while to realize how often music does it for me. Not just any music. Certain compositions. Certain chord progressions. A build-up that finally resolves. Sometimes it's subtle. Sometimes it hits like a wave. But once I noticed it, I started recognizing the same feeling in other places too. A line of dialogue in a film. A specific kind of tension in a scene. The rhythm of something that's been building and finally breaks loose.

That's the thread.

We all have them. Moments where our body responds before our brain does. Where emotion skips the filter. Most people feel it and move on. But if you stop and track it, if you slow down and really ask yourself what just happened, you'll start to uncover your blueprint.

It might be tied to sound. Or movement. Or connection. Or risk. It might come from creation or conflict or beauty or fear. But there are common themes. And if you can find yours, you can start setting your life up to step into them more often.

Because goosebumps aren't just some emotional static. They're feedback. Your nervous system's way of saying, "That meant something." Once you recognize the patterns, the hunt becomes easier. And the more you chase it, the more often it shows up.

That's not luck. That's awareness.

This isn't about chasing highs. It's not about cheap thrills or forcing meaning where there isn't any. It's about learning what speaks to you, and living in a way that puts you in front of it more often.

You've felt it before. That sudden stillness. That spike of energy. That chill that cuts through the noise and reminds you, for a split second, that you're alive. Don't wait for it to show up on accident. Build a life that invites it in.

It won't come from comfort. It won't come from scrolling. It won't come from playing it safe.

It comes from effort. From risk. From attention. From doing things that matter to you, even if no one else understands why.

If you're lucky, you'll figure out what gives you goosebumps. If you're disciplined, you'll build a life around it. Because that feeling, it's not just a reaction. It's a signal. A reminder that you're not here to watch life go by.

You're here to feel it.

Earn your goosebumps.

ON HAPPINESS

I was having a conversation with someone I care about deeply. It started as a disagreement, nothing dramatic, just one of those moments where two people are trying to navigate something real and not quite landing in the same place. Somewhere in the middle of it, this question came up: What is happiness?

Not what makes you happy, or what do you want out of life, but what actually is happiness?

We both stumbled on it. You'd think that's something we'd all be able to define, considering how often it gets talked about. But the more we tried to answer it, the more abstract it felt. Like we could recognize happiness when we experienced it, but putting it into words? That was a different story.

Later that night, I wrote it down on my phone: What is happiness?

I knew I wanted to come back to it. Not because I thought I'd find some universal truth, but because it felt worth unpacking. Slowly, honestly, and from a place that's been shaped more by experience than by theory. Not as a philosopher. Not as a therapist. Just as a man who's been through some things, and who wants to get this one right.

This is my attempt.

Once I started sitting with the question, I did what I usually do. I went to the source material. I started reading through what some of the old minds had to say. Not to copy their answers, but to see how people who actually spent their lives thinking about this stuff tried to define it.

I've always liked Stoicism. I've spent time reading Marcus Aurelius and Seneca, and a lot of what they say holds up.

They treated happiness not as a feeling, but as a kind of internal stability. A calm you earn by living with discipline, clarity, and self-control. That always resonated with me. It makes sense to put your energy into what you can control and not get spun up by the chaos around you. I've lived by that more often than not.

But even that didn't feel like the whole picture.

I kept digging. Aristotle talked about happiness as a kind of long-term fulfillment, only achieved through a life of virtue. Epicurus leaned into simplicity and the absence of pain. The Buddha talked about letting go of attachment altogether. Viktor Frankl said happiness isn't something you pursue. It's what shows up when your life has meaning. I could appreciate all of it. There's wisdom in those ideas.

Then I came across Nietzsche, and something clicked. He said happiness is the feeling that power increases, that resistance is being overcome. That stopped me for a second. Because I've felt that. I've felt something close to joy in the middle of hard moments. Not comfort. Not peace. Just that sense that I was pushing through something heavy and still moving forward. That what I was doing meant something.

And that was the first time I started to think that maybe happiness isn't supposed to feel soft. Maybe it's not the result of everything going right. Maybe it's what shows up when you're carrying real weight, doing something that matters, and you realize you haven't lost yourself in the process.

Still, as much as I respected the great thinkers, none of them gave me something I could carry forward on its own. None of them described happiness in a way that matched what I've seen and lived. That doesn't make their definitions wrong. It just meant I needed to keep going. The answer I was looking for wasn't going to come from a quote. It was going to have to come from experience.

After all the reading and reflection, I kept circling the same question. Not just what happiness is, but what it feels like when it's real. When you've lived through enough to know it's not just comfort or convenience. When you've seen the things that strip away illusions and still want to find something solid underneath.

Here's what I landed on.

> **Happiness is not the absence of struggle, but the presence of love, clarity, and strength. The kind that lets you wake up with purpose and still smile at the quiet moments.**

That's what made sense to me. It isn't soft. It isn't loud. It doesn't mean you're floating through life untouched by pain. It means you have something worth waking up for. You know what you believe in. You know who you care about. And even if the weight doesn't go away, you're strong enough to carry it and still feel some of it lift when you see someone you love smile for real.

There was a moment that brought this into focus for me. It came during one of the lowest points in my life. A stretch of time where I was barely holding it together, just surviving one miserable day at a time. But even then, I wasn't alone. I was fortunate to have someone beside me who had known me before it all came apart. She stayed through the worst of it.

One night, we were watching some show where a hotel maid folded the edge of a toilet paper roll into one of those neat little triangles. We both laughed and wondered why anyone bothers doing that. I said something like, maybe it's just a small way to show effort. A sign that if someone cares enough to do the little things right, they probably care about the big things too.

A few mornings later, after a night where I'd barely slept and a week where I couldn't afford much more than cheap groceries and pride, I got up before dawn to head out for work. And there it was. The edge of the toilet paper roll had been folded into a triangle.

It broke me. Not because of what it was, but because of what it meant. In the middle of all that pressure and survival mode, someone I loved had taken the time to do something so small and thoughtful, just so I'd see it. It hit me harder than any gesture ever had. I felt seen, cared for, and for the first time in a long time, like I might actually be okay. It was the most overwhelming feeling of love I'd experienced, all wrapped up in something so simple it could have been missed.

I don't think I said anything about it at the time. I just stood there in that tiny bathroom, half-awake, holding back tears. It was one of those moments that doesn't need to be talked through. You just feel it. And somehow, even in the middle of one of the worst stretches of my life, I felt loved. Fully, unmistakably loved.

That person is no longer with us. But that moment has stayed with me. Not just because of what it said about her, but because of what it revealed about happiness. It doesn't always show up in the big scenes. Sometimes it's a quiet act in the dark, meant to be found by someone trying to pull themselves together before the sun comes up.

This version of happiness doesn't reject hardship. It just refuses to let hardship be the only story. It leaves space for laughter in the middle of chaos. For gratitude after loss. For connection in the middle of fatigue.

It's not about being in control of everything. It's about being at peace with what you're carrying, and who you're becoming while you carry it.

For me, that's what happiness is. And once I finally saw it for what it was, it didn't feel vague anymore. It felt earned.

I don't claim to have figured this out. I don't think anyone really does. All I know is that I've spent time with the question. I've lived through enough to know that happiness isn't simple, and it definitely isn't one-size-fits-all. What makes me feel anchored might not land the same way for anyone else, and that's okay. That's part of the point.

Your definition won't be mine. It shouldn't be. Happiness looks different depending on who you are, what you've carried, and what you value when everything else falls away. For some people, it's peace. For others, it's forward motion. For some, it's the absence of pain. For others, it's the presence of love, even when the pain is still there.

What I've shared here isn't a theory or a set of instructions. It's just one person's attempt to understand something that's easy to feel, but hard to put into words. I started down this path because the question came up in a conversation that meant something to me. It stuck with me. So I followed it.

Maybe that's all this is...a place to begin.

This is my attempt.

What's yours?

BEAUTY IN THE BROKEN PLACES

Most people go out of their way to avoid taking damage. They avoid discomfort, failure, and anything that might leave a mark, as if staying clean is the goal. Somewhere along the line, they were convinced that looking untouched meant they were doing something right. But the truth is, it usually means they haven't done much at all.

The ones worth listening to are never spotless. They've been through it. Some of it left scars. Some of it changed how they think. None of it was easy. But that's where the value is. Not in the polish, but in the places that got roughed up and kept going anyway.

This isn't about chasing hardship or pretending pain is noble. It's about understanding that experience has a cost, and that the bill usually comes due in skin, sleep, and the quiet burden of lessons learned the hard way. People who have done meaningful things don't come away from them unscathed. They come away with stories, caution, and the kind of wisdom you can't get from a book. They also carry trauma. Some of it healed clean. Some of it didn't. But every piece of it shapes who they are now.

I've spent a lot of time trying to figure out the best way to explain this. Not just the concept of being tested, but what it actually means to come through those tests with something to show for it. That was the starting point for what became Earned Edges. It's not a slogan, and it's definitely not just about physical grit. It's about what we go through, what it costs us, and what we become because of it.

The idea started with injuries. I could look at the damage, things I broke, strained, or lost over the years, and remember exactly how it happened and what I learned from it. But the more I sat with it, the more I realized that the deeper marks weren't on the surface at all. They were the times I failed someone I cared about. The moments I doubted myself when I shouldn't have. The times I walked through something brutal and came out quieter, but more solid.

Those marks, physical or otherwise, aren't signs that something went wrong. They're reminders. That you didn't back down when it mattered. That you were tested, and you held the line, even if you were afraid or outmatched. They're proof that you've lived with intention, not just motion.

That's what Earned Edges means to me. It's a way of seeing the world that puts value where it belongs, not in how untouched you are, but in how deeply you've lived.

I think some of this started with my father.

He worked in one of the most competitive environments imaginable, the kind where there are only a handful of positions in the entire country, and every one of them is under a microscope. There was no real safety net, no long runway to fail and recover. You either performed or you were replaced. And even when you did everything right, new leadership could come in and level the entire operation overnight. That was the reality. You didn't earn comfort. You earned the right to keep your job a little longer.

He started at the very bottom, just trying to find a way in. Over time, through nothing but determination, discipline, and consistency, he climbed. It wasn't quick. It wasn't glamorous. It was the kind of climb that leaves marks, on your body, on your personal life, and on the way you see the world. But he never stopped. He kept showing up. And eventually, he worked his way to the top of a field where very few ever even get a foot in the door.

What stuck with me most weren't the titles or the perks, but the stories he told, quiet, matter-of-fact accounts of moments that would've broken most people. Times when people turned on him. Projects that failed. Entire organizations that fell apart. But no matter what, he kept moving forward with a kind of relentless structure and calm. Not robotic, just solid. Intentional. The kind of guy who didn't say "I'm trying my best," because he already was.

I remember going to work with him sometimes, seeing how he carried himself in rooms full of people who were all trying to survive in an environment designed to replace you the moment you slowed down. And he never did. He never stopped giving a damn. Whether it was running meetings or handling the small details no one else noticed, he approached every task with pride. Not the showy kind. The kind that says, "If my name's on it, it's going to be done right."

That left an impression on me. Probably more than I realized at the time.

He didn't talk about resilience or grit. He just lived it. He earned every inch of progress by showing up, getting back up, and holding his standards no matter what was happening around him. That, to me, is where Earned Edges begins. With the people who never quit, even when no one's watching. Especially then.

It's easy to believe that the goal is comfort. That if you're doing things right, life should be smooth, and success should come without friction. But that belief robs people of what actually builds strength, resilience, and clarity. The truth is, most of what makes a person capable, truly capable, comes from the exact moments they would've rather avoided.

The job loss. The heartbreak. The failure. The surgery. The injury. The thing you thought might break you but didn't. Those are the moments that carve the edges. Not because pain is something to worship, but because what you learn when everything hurts tends to stay with you longer than what you read in a book or heard in a podcast.

Edges don't just come from physical hardship. They come from having to navigate things that don't have a clear answer. They come from making decisions under pressure, from pushing forward when it would have been easier to disappear, and from doing things well even when no one is looking. The people who are worth having around in a crisis didn't learn how to be that way in a seminar. They learned because they had to. And they came out with the kind of calm that only shows up when you've been there before.

You don't have to go looking for pain, but you do have to stop running from anything that might test you. If you avoid every difficult conversation, every physical challenge, every uncomfortable truth, you may stay clean, but you'll never get sharp.

The goal isn't to become reckless or broken. The goal is to become shaped. Refined. Tough enough to face what's coming, and soft enough to remember why it matters. That balance isn't given. It's earned. And it only shows up in people who've done the work.

If you looked at my life from the outside, you might think I figured something out. Maybe you'd assume I had a plan that worked. But the truth is, I've failed more times than I can count. Not little stumbles, full-blown collapses. Some of them were my fault. Some of them weren't. Either way, I've had to rebuild more than once.

I've tried a lot of things. Started businesses. Taken risks. Lost money. Made it back. Lost it again. Trusted people I shouldn't have. Carried responsibilities I wasn't ready for. Walked into things with confidence and walked away humbled. There are times I've felt like I've lived five different lives in one body. And none of them were easy.

But I wouldn't trade a second of it.

Not for comfort. Not for convenience. Not even for peace. Because every one of those losses taught me something I couldn't have learned any other way. Every time I hit the floor, I came back a little sharper. A little quieter. A little less naive. Those moments, as ugly and exhausting as they were, did something that nothing else could. They shaped my edges.

Physically, I've got more injuries than I care to list. Some came from training. Some from accidents. Some just from doing what had to be done. And mentally, I've had to work through trauma that never fully leaves. It stays with you. Not like a scar, but like a change in how you see the world. There are things I've felt that I don't ever want to feel again. And there are things I've survived that make it nearly impossible for someone to lie to me, manipulate me, or sell me on a version of the world that isn't real.

That's the trade. You go through enough, and eventually, you stop needing to guess what's true. You just know.

And that's the foundation. Before you can talk about earning your edges, you have to understand what they really are. They aren't badges or stories to impress people. They're the armor you built one failure at a time. They're the reason you can spot danger when others are still debating it. They're why you don't panic when the room goes quiet or the plan falls apart.

You can't fake that. You have to live it.

If there's a cheat code, it's this: experience is earned, not learned.

You can't watch enough podcasts or listen to enough motivational speakers to bypass the actual work. You can't download someone else's pain, shortcut their failures, or absorb their lessons by osmosis. It doesn't matter how many times you hear a story about what not to do. You'll probably do it anyway. And that's exactly how it should be.

This has always been the price. Long before anyone had a job title or a resume, we made sharp things by breaking them. You took a stone, struck it hard, and chipped away everything dull until the edge could be used. The more useful the blade, the more broken it had to become first. That lesson is old, and still true.

There's no shortage of people trying to sell you the idea that their scars can keep you from getting your own. Guys like Ed Mylett, David Goggins, or whoever is making the rounds this month will tell you that if you just follow their blueprint, you can skip the hard parts. But that's not how it works. You don't become capable by copying someone else's path. You become capable by surviving your own.

Experience costs what it costs. The only choice you get is whether you pay that price willingly or get dragged through it.

So if you want to earn your edges and really earn them. Start here:

DO HARD THINGS BEFORE YOU'RE READY.
If you wait until the timing is perfect, you'll never move. Most of the people you admire didn't feel prepared when they started. They just went anyway. Starting before you're ready doesn't mean being reckless, it means accepting that readiness is often a myth people use to justify standing still.

TAKE RESPONSIBILITY FOR SOMETHING THAT MATTERS.
Not because someone told you to. Because you chose to. Find something that would fall apart if you let it, and carry it well. It could be your health. A business. A kid. A family member. A community. Responsibility forces you to grow

up faster than comfort ever will.

STOP OUTSOURCING YOUR PROBLEMS.
Don't wait for someone to save you. Don't blame the world. When something goes wrong, ask what part you played in it, even if your only mistake was trusting the wrong person or failing to prepare. That kind of thinking builds clarity, and clarity builds capability.

SEEK FRICTION, NOT CHAOS.
You don't need to blow up your life to grow. You just need resistance. Train. Build a new skill. Put yourself in rooms where you're the least experienced person there. Go somewhere you've never been. Try something that might not work. That's where the edges get carved.

REFLECT OFTEN. LIE NEVER.
You can go through hard things and still come out empty if you refuse to be honest. Every mistake is wasted if you don't sit with it long enough to understand what it cost you, and why you'll never do it again. Pain is a powerful teacher, but only if you're willing to listen.

You don't earn your edges by accident. You earn them by choosing the harder path when the easy one would've been enough. By showing up when it would have been easier to stay quiet. By holding the line when no one is watching.

The reality is, no one is coming to hand you resilience. No one can wrap experience in a box and drop it at your feet. You have to live it. You have to endure it. And you have to let it change you without hardening you into something bitter or broken.

The world doesn't reward potential. It rewards persistence. It rewards the ones who keep showing up after it would've made sense to quit. The ones who are tired, beat up, maybe even afraid, but still get back in the fight because they know who they are and what they're trying to build.

That's what the edges represent. Not damage. Not decoration. But proof. That you've been there. That you've earned your clarity, your confidence, and your competence through effort no one else saw and lessons no one else could have lived for you.

There are a thousand people right now offering you shortcuts, promising that their advice will keep you from falling into the same traps they did. But advice doesn't replace impact. Guidance is useful, but growth still costs what it costs. It always will.

Which brings me back to one of the best things I've ever read. A reminder I go back to every time things start to feel heavy:

> **Nothing in this world can take the place of persistence. Talent will not. Nothing is more common than unsuccessful men with talent. Genius will not. Unrewarded genius is almost a proverb. Education will not. The world is full of educated derelicts. Persistence and determination alone are omnipotent.**
> —Calvin Coolidge

When the dust settles, it won't be your credentials, your opinions, or your potential that matter. It will be your persistence. It will be your ability to stay in the fight, adapt, and hold your ground when it would have been easier to fold.

And if you're marked from it, if your body aches when it rains, if your thoughts sometimes drift into places that feel a little darker, if your past still echoes from time to time, that doesn't mean you're broken.

It means you've carried something real.

So the next time your knee hurts while you're walking, or something small triggers a memory you thought you had put away, don't hide from it. Don't apologize for it. Be proud of it. Those are reminders that you've lived with intention, that you've endured things that forged you into someone better. Not softer. Not harder. Just real.

That's what earns the edge. That's what builds someone who can be trusted when everything else is falling apart.

And if you're a little scraped, a little worn, a little scarred from the weight of all you've carried—that's not a sign you've done something wrong.

It's a sign you're doing it right.

THE EDGE REMAINS

The stone is never shaped by accident. Every ridge, every scar, every sharp line is the record of pressure applied and endured. Life works the same way. Every edge you carry was earned by contact with fear, responsibility, failure, and weight you could not put down. When everything else fades, the edge remains.

That edge does not come from a single lesson. It is the accumulation of strikes. No one wakes up with scars that mean something, and you do not inherit edges the way you inherit a last name. They are carved through contact, and the bill is paid in discomfort.

This book opened with that truth. Hold an arrowhead and you can read the story of every strike that shaped it. We are no different.

I think about anxiety first, because it is one of the edges most people try to hide. They imagine it is weakness, something to bury or manage in silence. Yet the quiet moments after the crisis passes reveal whether you are sharp. I learned the hard way that anxiety is rarely random. It echoes unfinished business, avoided responsibility, ducked conversations, and fears left unnamed. For years I treated it like background static until I realized it was a signal, and signals can be tracked.

Once I started facing what I wanted to avoid, the edge began to sharpen. I learned to fly instead of fearing the plane. I dove instead of running from deep water. Anxiety does not survive direct contact. It retreats when you move toward it, not away. The first edge many people earn is the ability to sit in silence without flinching, to face what gnaws instead of running from it.

Edges without purpose are decoration. Responsibility gives them weight. You can be as capable as you want in isolation, but if you never shoulder anything beyond yourself, you are sharp for show. What you protect reveals who you are. I have seen men step up without hesitation, not because they were fearless, but because they understood their role. They knew what was theirs to answer for, and they carried it. That instinct is ancient. It is not performance. It is the quiet promise that when the line is crossed, you will be the one who steps forward. I have carried responsibilities I was not ready for and answered for mistakes I could not hide. I have also felt the erosion that comes when responsibility slides. The truth does not change. What you protect defines you, and that edge does not dull.

Capability cuts from a different angle. Comfort dulls people faster than almost anything else. I have lost track of how often I have heard someone brag about what they cannot do, as if helplessness is a badge. I remember a night in a cigar bar in Boca Raton, talking with a friend about how hard it is to hang a commercial-grade door. It takes an eye for weight, structure, and alignment, the kind of judgment you only learn by doing. My friend Domsky, who has since passed away, taught me that years before. A man at the bar overheard us and laughed. "I have a guy for that," he said, as if helplessness proved sophistication. All I saw was fragility. Capability matters. Not because you must do everything yourself, but because when things break, when systems fail, when the guy does not answer his phone, you still have to be enough. You do not need to be a master of every trade. You need to be the kind of person who can figure it out. Quiet competence is an edge the world needs back.

Leadership sharpened me in a way nothing else could. It is easy to imagine leadership as authority or titles. Real leadership is the standard you set, the clarity you bring, and the line you refuse to let fade. I learned, often the hard way, that silence is not agreement, that people will nod while drifting unless you pull the truth into the light. After-action reports matter when things go right and when they go wrong, because trust is built on clarity, not on hope.

Credibility comes when you carry the weight before you ask anyone else to. Those lessons cut deep. They carve edges in you and in the people around you. A good leader makes others sharper by refusing to lower the standard. Those edges last long after the title is gone.

Then there is persistence, the deciding strike. I have watched talent fall away, intelligence stall, and education turn into excuses. What outlasts them all is the person who refuses to quit. Persistence is not glamorous. It does not shout. It looks like showing up again and again when no one cares, when the outcome is uncertain, when failure feels personal. My friend Curtis proved that to me. I did not come into the defense world through the front door. I started without pedigree or a sensible résumé. He saw the persistence, the clawing forward, the refusal to go away. He gave me a chance, not a handout, only an opening. That chance changed my life. He was killed in the line of duty in 2017. I will not stop trying to live up to the example he set. That is persistence made flesh, relentless, loyal, unshakable. His edge remains, even in death.

My mother taught the same truth from a different angle. After my parents divorced, she had to restart from zero. Years as a stay-at-home mother were behind her, and the structure she had built her life around was gone. Starting over at that stage was humbling. She began as a secretary and carried weight that would have crushed many people. She never quit. Day by day and year by year she climbed until she reached the executive level of a major company. I did not understand the cost or the grit it required until later. The distance she covered, from nothing to the top, is a map of what real persistence looks like.

I think of my father as well. He entered one of the most competitive environments imaginable, where you perform or you are replaced. He started at the bottom with no safety nets and clawed upward until he stood at the top of a field where very few even get in the door. He did not preach resilience. He lived it. Quietly and relentlessly, through titles, setbacks, and changes in leadership, he showed up. Discipline, standards, pride in doing things right. The titles faded. The edge did not.

These lessons are not separate. Anxiety, responsibility, capability, leadership, and persistence braid into the same arrowhead. Each strike sharpens a different facet. Together they form an edge that cannot be faked. You saw it in Carlos's story, standing in line behind a man complaining about his flight. Carlos looked at him and said, "It is your fault. You did not make enough money to fly private." Harsh words, but sharp ones, because ownership is the edge that changes everything. The moment you take responsibility, you stop bleeding power. You stop waiting for someone else to fix things. You stop drifting. That is how edges are made.

None of this is abstract. It shows up in details that look small until they are not. Most people do not fall in a single collapse. They leak away, one avoided detail at a time. They stop noticing tone in a relationship. They skip the gear check before an operation. They delay the response in a business deal. Smooth surfaces hide cracks until the whole thing gives way. The reverse is also true. Stability grows out of quiet repetitions, the habits no one celebrates. The edge is not formed by dramatic gestures. It is carved by a hundred small decisions stacked over years. That is what makes someone dependable when everything else falls apart.

Step back and look at the arc. Every page before this one has been a strike. Some landed in silence, some in noise, some in stories about loss and failure and persistence. Each left a mark. Together they formed a shape. When the storm comes, no one will ask what you meant to be. They will see only the edge you bring.

The storm will come. It will not arrive with music or warning. It will come in the conversation you have avoided. It will come in the unexpected loss. It will come in the responsibility you thought you were not ready to carry. It will come when comfort evaporates and no one else steps forward. In that moment there is no time for intention. Only edges. They are not built in the moment. They are revealed.

This is the point. Not whether you avoided scars, but whether you used them. Not whether you stayed smooth, but whether you stayed sharp. The world will not care about your potential or the version of yourself you hoped to become. It will care about the edge you bring when it counts.

So sharpen yourself. Not in theory. In contact. In struggle. In persistence. In the silence where anxiety lives. In the weight of responsibility. In the competence of capability. In the clarity of leadership. In the persistence that refuses to quit. Sharpen yourself until it becomes identity. Until no one wonders whether you will show up, because they already know.

When everything else is stripped away, when the noise dies, when comforts rot, when the applause is gone and even memory begins to fade, the edge remains. The world will not see polish. It will see scars. It will see proof. It will see a life that was shaped, not spared. That is what endures.

ACKNOWLEDGMENTS

I want to start by thanking my father, the one who gave me the courage to even attempt this. He told me to write this book, offered to help in any way possible, and reminded me that sometimes a simple vote of confidence is all you need. He's been a best friend and a rock, always steady and always present, and his push to put these words down meant more than I can say. My mother deserves the same gratitude, for showing me what love, support, and hard work look like day after day. She rebuilt her life from scratch and still kept family at the center of everything, a daily reminder of compassion and persistence. My sister has been in my corner the whole way, my hype woman, someone I've always been proud of. Watching her build an incredible family with Tom, raising Olive, and now getting ready to welcome another niece into the world, reminds me just how much strength and joy she carries. And my grandmother—no matter where I was, far or near, she was always there, always listening, always excited, always on my side. That kind of love doesn't fade, and I carry it with me.

To my closest friends, I owe just as much. Aaron, you're the reason I even started writing. Before ISG, my best attempt at an article was bullet points and voice-to-text, but building that community with you lit a fire. Working together over the years has been an absolute gift, and there's no one else I'd rather have watching my back. You're a shining example of a father, and a man who embodies everything this book is meant to capture. Matt, you've been my best friend since childhood and one of the greatest minds I've ever known. Your accomplishments are endless, but more than that, you've been an incredible business partner and an even better friend. Standing beside you as your best man was one of the highlights of my life, and I can't wait to see what the future brings you. Stephen, you've been there since the beginning—through adventures, through life at full tilt, never hesitating to jump in and live. You're a hell of a wingman, and I look forward to all the miles we haven't logged yet. And Carlos, you've taught me more about business and people than anyone else, always the first to listen to my ideas, always the first to point out how I could get screwed, and always the one to push me to sharpen them into something better. You've been an incredible friend, a wealth of knowledge, and a man whose dedication to his family I deeply respect.

I know there are others who aren't named here, but I didn't forget you. If you've been part of my life, if you've shaped me in ways big or small, you're in these pages too. And to all of you—the ones I've named and the ones I hold just as close—I want you to know this: I hope I've done you proud. Every word I've written carries the weight of what you've given me. Your love, your guidance, your friendship, your belief—it means the world to me. This book may have my name on the cover, but it belongs to all of us.

www.ingramcontent.com/pod-product-compliance
Lightning Source LLC
Chambersburg PA
CBHW050912160426
43194CB00011B/2379